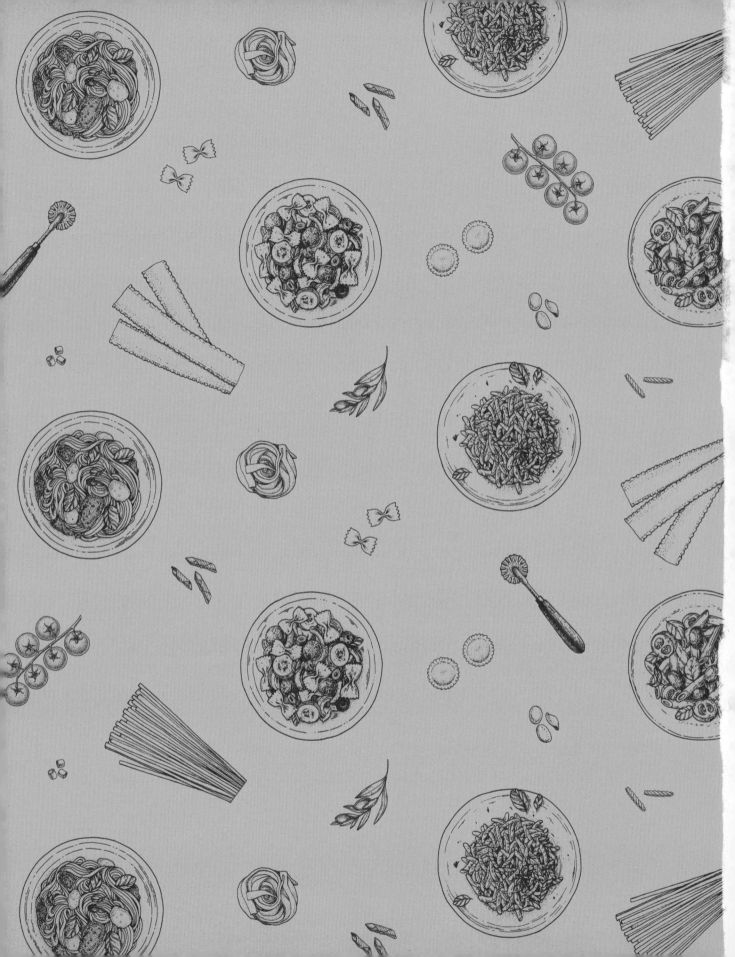

PASTA

This book may be ordered by mail from the publisher. Please include $5.99 for postage and handling. Please support your local bookseller first!

Books published by Cider Mill Press Book Publishers are available at special discounts for bulk purchases in the United States by corporations, institutions, and other organizations. For more information, please contact the publisher.

Cider Mill Press Book Publishers
"Where good books are ready for press"
PO Box 454
12 Spring Street
Kennebunkport, Maine 04046

Visit us online!
cidermillpress.com

Typography: Adobe Garamond Pro, Black Jack, Gotham, Type Embellishments One

Image Credits: Photos on pages 30, 36, 39, 41, 42, 46, 57, 74, 78, 101, 109, 113, 118, 121, 122, 125, 127, 128, 131, 134, 138, 141, 142, 145, 149, 153, 154, 161, 166, 169, 171, 182, 217, and 222 courtesy of Cider Mill Press.
All other images used under official license from Shutterstock.com.

Back cover image:
Lamb Ragù, see page 84.

Front endpaper image:
Sweet Potato Gnocchi, see page 48.

Back endpaper image:
Butternut Squash Ravioli, see page 136.

Printed in China
1 2 3 4 5 6 7 8 9 0
First Edition

PASTA

Over 100 Recipes for Fresh, Homemade Noodles, Dumplings, and More

CIDER MILL
PRESS

BOOK
PUBLISHERS

KENNEBUNKPORT, MAINE

TABLE *of* CONTENTS

∽

INTRODUCTION

⚮

Versatile, wholesome, and inexpensive, pasta was destined to become beloved. Providing the proverbial blank canvas upon which some of the world's most popular dishes are crafted, it is the rare item that can withstand any shift in taste and accommodate every culinary trend. Blessing each plate or bowl it graces with feelings of comfort and care, pasta has transcended its humble composition (flour, eggs, and water) to become a cornerstone of the modern diet.

As the increasingly hectic pace of the world beckons us away from the kitchen, pasta is a tie to the vital and enriching act of taking a step back to provide sustenance for our loved ones and ourselves. There are days when concocting a meal is the last thing one wants to think about, but thanks to pasta's adaptability and ease of preparation, it always provides a way past this apprehension.

Since the affection for all things pasta is undeniable, we thought it would be well worth fueling the fire. With instructions on how to whip up fresh noodles, comforting soups, indulgent dishes, silky sauces, and more, we're certain that even the most zealous pasta enthusiast will find something to warm their heart.

Dig in. You'll soon see why we believe that pasta, in its various forms, is one of the best testaments to humanity's limitless creativity and ingenuity.

MAKING YOUR OWN PASTA

❧

Making your own pasta is not rocket science. At the end of the day, it can be as simple as combining two ingredients, eggs and flour, or flour and water. Should you decide to use the all-purpose flour in your pantry and high-quality eggs, you'll make pasta more delicious than anything you could purchase from the market, even those from high-end grocers.

If, on the other hand, you would like to delve deeper into understanding the subtleties of the ingredients that go into pasta making, read on. Once you begin experimenting with different types of flour and ingredients you will quickly be able to discern the slightest of differences, which is a profoundly satisfying development.

FLOUR: THE FOUNDATION OF PASTA

❧

A passion for making great pasta translates into a knowledge of flour. There's no way around it. Otherwise, it's akin to trying to master the piano without understanding anything about chord structure.

To understand how flour will aid in your pasta-making exploits, it is important to recognize the role protein plays in flour and how it affects the dough. Once water is added to flour and the kneading process begins, proteins come into contact and form a bond that creates a network of fine strands in the dough known as gluten. This network is what gives dough its structure and strength.

In the seminal book *On Food and Cooking,* author and food scientist Harold McGee relates that the Chinese call gluten "the muscle of flour." It is an apt description, as gluten gives dough its elasticity and plasticity, which is the ability to take on a shape and keep it. The right amount of gluten results in a pasta dough that is easier to knead, put through the pasta maker, and stretch without tearing when handled. This explains why bread flour contains higher amounts of protein and why pasta noodles, which need to be more malleable, require less.

WHEAT

❧

For thousands of years the wheat plant crossbred arbitrarily with other plants and grasses, evolving into several different species. One of them, *Triticum aestivum,* proved particularly desirable because it contains glutenin, which produced a more elastic and malleable dough that was easier to shape.

Humans began to cultivate this particular species more than 8,000 years ago and it now accounts for 90 percent of the wheat grown around the world.

Within the T. aestivum genus, wheat is generally categorized by whether it is hard or soft, red or white, winter or spring. For the purposes of this book, we will focus on flours that tend to fall within the red (more flavorful, or "wheatier"), soft (less gluten, resulting in more malleable dough), and winter (slightly less gluten than spring) categories, as they tend to produce better tasting pasta that has a chewy yet tender texture.

Accounting for most of the remaining 10 percent of world's wheat production is *Triticum durum*, also known as durum wheat. Similar to T. aestivum, it originated in the Middle East and spread to many parts of the Mediterranean Basin before the spread of the Roman Empire. Deep amber in color and rich in protein, durum wheat is ground into semolina flour and used to make almost all of the dry pasta that is sold commercially. Durum wheat is considerably different from other grains because its flour contains the gluten protein gliadin, which is extensible rather than elastic. This means that its dough can be rolled easily into sheets, that the resulting pasta dries without breaking, and can reliably hold intricate shapes.

Before we begin exploring the different flours used in pasta making, it is worth noting that flour is not a static product. If "a rose is a rose is a rose" in Gertrude Stein's world, then "flour is not flour is not flour" in ours. In other words, the bag of flour in your pantry is probably very different from your next-door neighbor's. In fact, flour varies greatly depending on whether it comes from a nearby mill, a regional manufacturer, or a nationally recognized one. That's because when flour is milled, its composition, and thus performance, depends on the wheat grain variety, growing season, the soil in which it is grown, protein content, milling technique, temperature of the grain at the time of milling, and storage. National brands are the exception. Blended specifically for consistency, they combine different hard and soft wheat varieties to guarantee certain protein-level compositions. Because of this, they are often the flour of choice among professional bakers, who value predictability and consistency above all else.

Ultimately, the decision on what flour to use is yours. As mentioned earlier, fresh pasta made with a national brand of flour and good quality eggs will be delicious. Its only shortcoming will be its neutral flavor, which will contain none of the aromatic notes of nuts, tobacco, and even grass that you would find in a freshly milled flour.

Unbleached All-Purpose Flour: Typically produced from a blend of hard, high-protein bread flours and soft, low-protein pastry flours, all-purpose flour contains a moderate level of protein that ranges from 9 percent to 12 percent in national flour brands but can go as low as

7.5 percent in small regional brands. Blended and milled to be versatile, it is strong enough to make bread and soft enough to create tender, delicate scones, cakes, and biscuits. It also makes perfectly tender pasta, though combining it with other flours such as semolina results in tastier and slightly firmer noodles. Avoid bleached flour whenever possible, as it is treated with chemicals like benzoyl peroxide and chlorine gas to speed up the flour's aging process. The unbleached version is aged naturally, through oxidation.

"00" Flour: Produced from soft wheat, and ground so fine it is almost talcum-like, "00" flour is fairly low in protein content. It is the flour of choice in most Italian homes because it produces soft dough that is easy to roll and yields pastas and noodles that are smooth and silky. Tender egg pastas such tagliatelle, garganelli, and corzetti have most likely been prepared with a dough made from "00" flour and eggs. Occasionally the categorization of "00" flour causes some confusion because despite always being finely milled into powdery form, it can be made from soft or hard varieties of wheat and consequently contains different percentages of protein by weight. Soft wheat is lower in protein and creates soft and tender pasta that readily absorbs and takes on the flavor of a tasty sauce. Hard wheat is higher in protein content and creates a sturdy dough that is ideal for trapping air bubbles, like bread dough, but that quality makes it almost impossible to roll into sheets for pasta. When purchasing it, you will find "00" flour designated for bread and pizza or for pasta, with protein contents ranging from 5 percent to 12 percent. Be sure to select a "00" flour toward the lower end of this range (or one specifically designated for making pasta). If this flour is not readily available in your area, it is only a click away on the internet.

Semolina Flour and Durum Flour: Both of these come from milling durum wheat berries, which have the highest protein content. Semolina comes from milling the innermost layer, called the endosperm, of the berry. It is characteristically coarse and golden in color as a result of its high concentration of carotenoids (the same compounds responsible for the carrot's bright orange color). It creates a strong pasta dough that holds any shape and strengthens when heated. Experienced pasta makers often add small amounts of semolina flour to pasta dough made predominantly with "00" flour to add a pleasant chewiness and subtle nutty flavor, as well as increase the dough's elasticity during rolling. Semolina flour also makes an excellent alternative to cornmeal, and can be used to dust formed pasta and work surfaces intended for pasta making. As the word *semolina* is also used to describe the innermost layer of any grain, such as corn and rice, some confusion can arise when people encounter this term.

Durum flour has a very fine texture that makes it look like golden all-purpose flour. A byproduct of milling semolina flour, it creates a malleable pasta dough that is easily fed through pasta makers and will curl or bend during cooking. Again, if either of these flours is not readily available in your area, look for it online.

Whole Wheat Flour: This flour is ground from the entire wheat berry of either hard red spring or winter wheat: the endosperm, germ, and bran. Brown in color and lightly speckled, whole wheat adds a full-bodied wheaty flavor that, due to the tannins in the outer bran, can at times verge on bitterness. Chock-full of naturally occurring vitamins, minerals, and fiber, it is a viable option for health-oriented individuals who don't mind its assertive flavor. For best results, it is advisable to add some all-purpose flour to your dough to make it more pliable and the pasta more tender. Whole wheat flour also tends to absorb more moisture than white flour, so you'll need to adjust for that if you're substituting it in a recipe. There is also white whole wheat flour, which is ground from hard white spring or winter wheat berries; it possesses the same nutritional profile as whole wheat flour but is milder in flavor and lighter in color.

EGGS: TENDER PASTA'S NOT-SO-SECRET INGREDIENT

For the purposes of making pasta, and eating the most wholesome food possible, it is best to secure the highest quality eggs available to you.

Eggs play a vital role in many fresh pasta recipes. Not only do they enrich the noodles from a nutritional standpoint, they also add an appealing pale yellow color and a subtle flavor to the dough. Eggs also contribute two additional elements that may be more important to a pasta maker. First, they provide more protein, which, when combined with the gluten in the dough, enhances its structure, making the dough elastic, soft, and easier to roll out thin without tearing. Secondly, the egg whites provide additional heft and firmness to the dough while preventing the loss of starch as the pasta cooks.

It is important to use eggs that have a vibrantly orange yolk, as it is a sign of a healthy, happy, and well-fed chicken. Egg yolks get their color from carotenoids, which are also responsible for strengthening the chicken's immune system. Because chickens only hatch eggs if they have sufficient levels of carotenoids, the yolks possess deep hues of dark gold and orange. Paler yolks are often a result of chickens feeding on barley or white cornmeal, foods that don't nourish them as thoroughly as a diet based on yellow corn and marigold petals.

Using brown or white eggs is up to the discretion of the individual, since they both share the same nutritional profiles and taste the same. Aliza Green, connoisseur and author of the wonderful book *Making Artisan Pasta,* makes a good argument for buying brown eggs. First, brown eggs come from larger breeds that eat more, take longer to produce their eggs, and produce eggs with thicker protective shells, which prevents internal moisture loss over time and helps maintain freshness.

Also, because brown eggs are considered a specialty product, she adds, their quality tends to be higher.

Eggs in the US are graded according to the thickness of their shell and the firmness of their egg whites. Agricultural advances have made it possible for large egg producers to assess the quality of each individual egg and to efficiently sort them by size, weight, and quality. With almost scientific precision, eggs are graded AA (top quality), A (good quality found in most supermarkets), and B (substandard eggs with thin shells and watery whites that don't reach consumers, but are used commercially and industrially). They are also further categorized by size: medium, large (the most common size), and extra large.

The past decade or so has also seen a rise in popularity of free-range and organic eggs. The product of smaller-scale enterprises, these chickens are given organic feed and are caged with slightly more space at their disposal than what is available on industrial-scale chicken farms. While the jury is still out on whether this last category tastes betters, it nonetheless constitutes an additional, and perhaps politically oriented, option for pasta makers.

For the purposes of making pasta, it is best to secure the freshest eggs available, so check the expiration dates before buying them and buy them when they are well within that window.

When making pasta it is important to avoid cold at all costs, so make sure to use room-temperature eggs. Also, do not work on a naturally cold surface such as marble or stainless steel. Wood is best; otherwise Corian or linoleum will work.

WATER

The water you use, its mineral content, and its temperature can impact the quality of your pasta dough.

Mineral-rich water from your tap is best for making pasta. The only exception is if your water is particularly hard, or excessively high in minerals like magnesium and calcium. In that case, you may be better off using spring water, as too much magnesium or calcium can produce a tighter gluten network in the dough and result in a firmer, and sometimes too firm, dough. Always use warm water, around 105°F (or two parts cold water to one part boiling water), as it makes it easier for the flour to absorb the liquid.

SALT

❦

Use fine-grain iodized salt (table salt) or slightly coarser kosher salt, as both work nicely and contribute a hint of salty flavor to your pasta. Try to avoid using sea salt in either fine or coarse-grained forms, as its high mineral content can cause dough to develop a tighter gluten network, resulting in a firmer, and sometimes too firm, noodle.

USING YOUR PASTA MAKER

❦

First, since you're enough of a pasta-phile to purchase a book built dedicated to it, we're assuming that you already have a pasta maker. But if not, better-than-satisfactory versions are available for around $40.

Once you have cut and rolled your dough, set the pasta maker for the flat roller (no teeth) on the widest setting (typically notch 1). Now feed the dough into the rollers. As a rather rough, thick sheet comes out the other end, make sure to support it with one of your hands. Fold the sheet of dough over itself twice, as you would a letter, and then turn the folded dough 90 degrees and feed it back through the pasta maker. Repeat this folding and feeding it back into the pasta maker three more times. This process is called "laminating" and it makes the dough more sturdy and manageable to handle.

Set the pasta maker to the second-widest setting (typically notch 2) and feed the dough into the rollers. Again, support the pasta as it comes out the other side. Fold it as you would a letter and feed it into the rollers. Repeat three additional times.

Set the pasta maker to the third-widest setting (typically notch 3) and feed the dough into the rollers. Again, support the pasta as it comes out the other side. Fold it as you would a letter and feed it into the rollers. Repeat three additional times.

Set the pasta maker to the second-smallest setting (typically notch 4). Feed the pasta into the rollers. Again, support the pasta as it comes out the other side. At this point, there is no need to laminate the pasta.

Stop rolling at this point if making sheets of pasta that are ⅛ inch thick for pansoti, agnolotti, maltagliati, farfalle, and cappellacci dei briganti. If you like your fettuccine, pappardelle, and tagliatelle a little thicker, then this is the setting for you.

If thinner sheets of pasta are desired, set the pasta maker to the smallest setting (typically notch 5). Cut the pasta sheet in half and feed it into the rollers. Again, support the pasta as it comes out the other side.

This last setting makes pasta sheets that are about $1/16$ inch thick—that's so thin you can see light through them. It is ideal for filled pastas like ravioli, ravioloni, tortellini, anolini, cappellacci di zucca, and caramelle, whose fillings can easily be overshadowed by too much surrounding dough, as well as fazzoletti and quadretti. If you like your fettuccine, pappardelle, and tagliatelle very thin, then this is the setting for you.

The just-rolled pasta will be very delicate, so be gentle handling it. If the pasta sheet is too long to easily handle, carefully cut it in half. Lightly dust each sheet with flour and lay it on a surface lined with wax or parchment paper. Repeat all the above steps with the remaining pieces of dough.

The dough needs to dry for approximately 15 minutes after it has been rolled out and before it is cut into strands or other shapes. This drying time makes the dough less sticky and easier to handle. Keep in mind that when the pasta is very thick or wide it will need to be turned over to ensure thorough and even drying (not necessary for thinner noodles). The notable exception to this rule is if you are making stuffed pasta. In this case, not letting the dough dry is best because the slight stickiness helps create a better seal.

Once fresh pasta has been cut, toss it with some semolina flour, place it on a semolina flour–dusted surface, and allow it to dry for at least 15 minutes before cooking. This drying period is important because it allows the pasta to become firmer and less sticky, which prevents the pasta from sticking together as it cooks (noodles also holds their shape better when allowed to dry slightly before cooking). More specific drying times are indicated in individual recipes. Just note that the drying process can be fickle. Depending on temperature, humidity levels, and the size of the noodles or pasta, the process may take a longer or shorter period of time than stated in the recipes. Also, it is probably best to avoid making pasta on very humid days. If you can't avoid it, turn on the air conditioner or even an oscillating fan to help the air circulate more effectively.

CHAPTER 1

DOUGHS & NOODLES

The dream of making fresh pasta is a common one.
It is a fantasy that is also frequently drowned out by the ease of
opening a box and dumping its contents into a pot of boiling water.
Too often, in our opinion. Because there's nothing out of reach about
fashioning a simple dough, letting it rest, and running it through
a pasta maker before cutting it into the desired shape.

Making your own pasta's not miraculous, it only tastes like it.
This chapter intends to introduce you to a few basic doughs that will help
you turn out classic noodles like spaghetti and linguine as well as a few
off-the-beaten path options that will soon become as cherished as those
standards. So start fresh, and shift pasta from a last-resort dish to
an immersive experience that everyone looks forward to.

YIELD: ¾ LB.

ACTIVE TIME: **20 MINUTES**

TOTAL TIME: **2 HOURS AND 30 MINUTES**

Basic Pasta Dough

INGREDIENTS

2¾ CUPS ALL-PURPOSE FLOUR, PLUS MORE AS NEEDED

3 LARGE EGGS

1 EGG YOLK

2 TABLESPOONS WARM WATER (105°F), PLUS MORE AS NEEDED

DIRECTIONS

1. Place the flour in a mixing bowl and form it into a mound. Create a well in the center and place the eggs, egg yolk, and the water in the well. Using a fork or your fingers, gradually start incorporating the flour into the well until the dough starts holding together in a single mass. Incorporate more water, 1 tablespoon at a time, if the mixture is too dry to hold together. Once the dough feels firm and dry and can be formed into a ball, it's time to start kneading.

2. Work any remaining flour into the ball of dough. Using the heel of your hand, push the ball of dough away from you. Turn the dough 45 degrees each time you repeat this motion, as doing so incorporates the flour more evenly. As you continue to knead, you'll notice the dough getting less and less floury. Eventually it will have a smooth, elastic texture. If the dough still feels wet or tacky, dust it with flour and continue kneading. If it feels too dry and is not completely sticking together, wet your hands with water and continue kneading. Wet your hands as many times as you need to until the dough is smooth and springy, about 8 to 10 minutes. The dough has been sufficiently kneaded when it gently pulls back when stretched.

3. Wrap the ball of dough tightly in plastic wrap and let it rest for 2 hours at room temperature. The dough will keep for up to 3 days in the refrigerator, but may experience some discoloration.

Continued...

4. Cut the dough into four even pieces. Set one piece on a smooth work surface and cover the rest in plastic wrap to prevent them from drying out. Shape the piece of dough into a ball, place it on the surface, and, with the palm of your hand, push down on it so that it looks like a thick pita. Using a rolling pin, roll the dough to ½ inch thick. Try as much as possible to keep the thickness and width of the dough even, as it will make it easier to fit the through the pasta maker. For instructions on running the dough through the pasta maker, see pages 15–16.

TIP: This dough is suitable for popular noodles such as fettuccine (¼ to ½ inch wide), pappardelle (1- to 1½-inch-wide), tagliatelle (¾ inch wide), and tortellini (see page 28).

All-Yolk Pasta Dough

INGREDIENTS

1½ CUPS ALL-PURPOSE FLOUR

⅓ CUP "00" FLOUR, PLUS MORE
AS NEEDED

8 LARGE EGG YOLKS

2 TABLESPOONS WARM WATER
(105°F), PLUS MORE AS NEEDED

DIRECTIONS

1. Place the flours in a mixing bowl and form the mixture into a mound. Create a well in the center and place the egg yolks and the water in the well. Using a fork or your fingers, gradually start incorporating the flour into the well until the dough starts holding together in a single mass. Incorporate more water, 1 tablespoon at a time, if the mixture is too dry to hold together. Once the dough feels firm and dry and can be formed into a ball, it's time to start kneading.

2. Work any remaining flour into the ball of dough. Using the heel of your hand, push the ball of dough away from you. Turn the dough 45 degrees each time you repeat this motion, as doing so incorporates the flour more evenly. As you continue to knead, you'll notice the dough getting less and less floury. Eventually it will have a smooth, elastic texture. If the dough still feels wet or tacky, dust it with flour and continue kneading. If it feels too dry and is not completely sticking together, wet your hands with water and continue kneading. Wet your hands as many times as you need to until the dough is smooth and springy, about 8 to 10 minutes. The dough has been sufficiently kneaded when it gently pulls back when stretched.

3. Wrap the ball of dough tightly in plastic wrap and let it rest for 2 hours at room temperature. The dough will keep for up to 3 days in the refrigerator, but may experience some discoloration.

    Continued...

4. Cut the dough into four even pieces. Set one piece on a smooth work surface and cover the rest in plastic wrap to prevent them from drying out. Shape the piece of dough into a ball, place it on the surface, and, with the palm of your hand, push down on it so that it looks like a thick pita. Using a rolling pin, roll the dough to ½ inch thick. Try as much as possible to keep the thickness and width of the dough even, as it will make it easier to fit the through the pasta maker. For instructions on running the dough through the pasta maker, see pages 15–16.

TIP: This dough is suitable for noodles such as lasagna, cannelloni, and tajarin, and should be used right away.

Whole Wheat Pasta Dough

YIELD: **¾ LB.**

ACTIVE TIME: **20 MINUTES**

TOTAL TIME: **2 HOURS AND 30 MINUTES**

INGREDIENTS

4 CUPS FINE WHOLE WHEAT
FLOUR, PLUS MORE AS NEEDED

1½ TEASPOONS SALT

4 LARGE EGG YOLKS

1 TABLESPOON OLIVE OIL

2 TABLESPOONS WATER, PLUS
MORE AS NEEDED

DIRECTIONS

1. In a mixing bowl or on a work surface, combine the flour and salt and form it into a mound. Create a well in the center and place the egg yolks, olive oil, and the water in the well. Using a fork or your fingers, gradually start incorporating the flour into the well until the dough starts holding together in a single mass. Incorporate more water, 1 tablespoon at a time, if the mixture is too dry to hold together. Once the dough feels firm and dry and can be formed into a ball, it's time to start kneading.

2. Work any remaining flour into the ball of dough. Using the heel of your hand, push the ball of dough away from you. Turn the dough 45 degrees each time you repeat this motion, as doing so incorporates the flour more evenly. As you continue to knead, you'll notice the dough getting less and less floury. Eventually it will have a smooth, elastic texture. If the dough still feels wet or tacky, dust it with flour and continue kneading. If it feels too dry and is not completely sticking together, wet your hands with water and continue kneading. Wet your hands as many times as you need to until the dough is smooth and springy, about 8 to 10 minutes. The dough has been sufficiently kneaded when it gently pulls back when stretched.

3. Wrap the ball of dough tightly in plastic wrap and let it rest for 2 hours at room temperature. The dough will keep for up to 3 days in the refrigerator, but may experience some discoloration.

   Continued...

4. Cut the dough into four even pieces. Set one piece on a smooth work surface and cover the rest in plastic wrap to prevent them from drying out. Shape the piece of dough into a ball, place it on the surface, and, with the palm of your hand, push down on it so that it looks like a thick pita. Using a rolling pin, roll the dough to ½ inch thick. Try as much as possible to keep the thickness and width of the dough even, as it will make it easier to run the dough through the pasta maker. For instructions on running the dough through the pasta maker, see pages 15–16.

TIP: This dough is perfect for those who are looking for a slightly chewier pappardelle or linguine. Whole wheat pasta is also great with thick, creamy sauces.

YIELD: **¾ LB.**

ACTIVE TIME: **30 MINUTES**

TOTAL TIME: **1 HOUR**

Ravioli

INGREDIENTS

2 CUPS "00" FLOUR, PLUS MORE
AS NEEDED

PINCH OF KOSHER SALT, PLUS
MORE TO TASTE

9 EGG YOLKS, BEATEN

2 TEASPOONS OLIVE OIL

1 EGG

1 TABLESPOON WATER

DIRECTIONS

1. Place the flour and salt in a mixing bowl, stir to combine, and make a well in the center. Place the egg yolks and olive oil in the well and slowly incorporate the flour until the dough holds together. Knead the dough until smooth, about 5 minutes. Cover the bowl with plastic wrap and let stand at room temperature for 30 minutes.

2. To form the ravioli, divide the dough into two pieces. Use a pasta maker to roll each piece into a long, thin rectangle. Place one of the rectangles over a flour-dusted ravioli tray and place a teaspoon of your desired filling into each of the depressions. Place the egg and water in a small bowl and beat until combined. Dip a pastry brush or a finger into the egg wash and lightly coat the edge of each ravioli with it. Gently lay the other rectangle over the piece of dough in the ravioli tray. Use a rolling pin to gently cut out the ravioli. Remove the cut ravioli and place them on a flour-dusted baking sheet.

3. To cook the ravioli, bring a large saucepan of water to a boil. When the water is boiling, add salt and the ravioli, stir to make sure they do not stick to the bottom, and cook until tender but still chewy, about 2 minutes.

Tortellini

INGREDIENTS

BASIC PASTA DOUGH (SEE PAGE 20)

SEMOLINA FLOUR, AS NEEDED

SALT, TO TASTE

DIRECTIONS

1. Prepare the dough as directed, rolling it to the thinnest setting (generally notch 5) for pasta sheets that are about ¹⁄₁₆ inch thick. Dust the sheets with flour, place them on flour-dusted, parchment-lined baking sheets, and cover with plastic wrap.

2. Working with one pasta sheet at a time, place it on a flour-dusted work surface and, using a round stamp or pastry cutter, cut as many 1¼-inch rounds or squares out of it as possible. Transfer the rounds or squares to flour-dusted, parchment-lined baking sheets and cover with plastic wrap. Repeat with all the pasta sheets. Gather the scraps together into a ball, put it through the pasta maker to create additional pasta sheets, and cut those as well.

3. Place ½ teaspoon of your desired filling in the center of each round or square. Lightly moisten the edge of the pasta with a fingertip dipped in water. Fold the dough over to form a half-moon or a triangle. Now draw the two corners together; if using a pasta round, this will form a nurse's cap; for a square, it will have a kerchief shape. Press down around the joined sides to create a tight seal. As you do this, try to push out any air from around the filling, which prevents the tortellini from coming apart in the water when boiling due to vapor pressure. Press one more time to ensure you have a tight seal. Dust with flour, place the sealed tortellini on baking sheets, and let them dry for 2 hours.

4. To cook the tortellini, place them in a large saucepan of boiling, salted water and cook until they are tender but still chewy, 2 to 3 minutes.

YIELD: **¾ LB.**

ACTIVE TIME: **1 HOUR**

TOTAL TIME: **3 HOURS AND 30 MINUTES**

Farfalle

INGREDIENTS

ALL-YOLK PASTA DOUGH
(SEE PAGE 22)

SEMOLINA FLOUR, AS NEEDED

SALT, TO TASTE

DIRECTIONS

1. Prepare the dough as directed, rolling the dough to the second thinnest setting (generally notch 4) for pasta sheets that are about ⅛ inch thick. Lay the pasta sheets on flour-dusted, parchment-lined baking sheets and cover loosely with plastic wrap. Work quickly to keep the pasta sheets from drying out, which makes it harder for the pasta to stick together.

2. Working with one pasta sheet at a time, place it on a flour-dusted work surface and trim both ends to create a rectangle. Using a pastry cutter, cut the pasta sheet lengthwise into 1- to 1¼-inch-wide ribbons. Carefully separate the ribbons from each other, then, using a ridged pastry cutter, cut the ribbons into 2-inch pieces. To form the butterfly shape, place the index finger of your weak hand on the center of the piece of pasta. Then place the thumb and index finger of your dominant hand on the sides of the rectangle, right in the middle, and pinch the dough together to create a butterfly shape. Firmly pinch the center again to help it hold its shape. Leave the ruffled ends of the farfalle untouched. Repeat with all the pasta sheets.

3. Set the farfalle on lightly floured, parchment-lined baking sheets so they are not touching. Allow them to air-dry for at least 30 minutes and up to 3 hours, and then cook. Alternatively, you can place them, once air-dried, in a bowl, cover with a kitchen towel, and refrigerate for up to 3 days. Or freeze on the baking sheets, transfer to freezer bags, and store in the freezer for up to 2 months. Do not thaw them prior to cooking (they will become mushy) and add an extra minute or so to their cooking time.

4. To cook the farfalle, bring a large pot of salted water to a boil. Add the farfalle and cook until the pasta is tender but still chewy, 2 to 3 minutes.

YIELD: **1 LB.**

ACTIVE TIME: **45 MINUTES**

TOTAL TIME: **4 HOURS**

Orecchiette

INGREDIENTS

2 CUPS SEMOLINA FLOUR, PLUS
MORE AS NEEDED

1 TEASPOON SALT, PLUS MORE
TO TASTE

¾ CUP WATER, PLUS MORE
AS NEEDED

DIRECTIONS

1. Combine the flour and salt in a large bowl. Add the water a little at a time and work the mixture with a fork until it starts holding together. If it is too dry to stick together, incorporate more water, 1 teaspoon at a time, until it does. Work the dough with your hands until it feels firm and dry and can be formed into a ball.

2. Transfer the dough to a flour-dusted work surface and knead it. Because it is made with semolina flour, the dough can be quite stiff and hard. You can also knead this in a stand mixer; don't try it with a handheld mixer— the dough will be too stiff and could burn the motor out. Using the heel of your hand, push the ball of dough away from you in a downward motion. Turn the dough 45 degrees each time you repeat this motion, as doing so incorporates the flour more evenly. Wet your hands as needed if the dough is too sticky. After 10 minutes of kneading, the dough will only be slightly softer (most of the softening is going to occur when the dough rests, which is when the gluten network within the dough will relax). Shape the dough into a ball, cover it tightly with plastic wrap, and let rest in the refrigerator for 2 hours.

3. Cut the dough into four equal pieces. Take one piece and shape it into an oval. Cover the remaining pieces with plastic wrap to prevent them from drying out. Place the dough on a flour-dusted work surface and roll it into a long, ½-inch-thick rope. Using a sharp paring knife, cut the rope into ¼-inch discs, dusting them with semolina flour so they don't stick together.

Continued...

4. To form the orecchiette, place a disc on the work surface. Dip your thumb in semolina flour, place it on top of the disc, and, applying a little pressure, drag your thumb across the dough to create an earlike shape. For best results, dip your thumb in semolina flour before making each orecchiette. Dust the formed orecchiette with flour and set them on flour-dusted, parchment-lined baking sheets, making sure they are not touching. Let them dry for 1 hour, turning them over once halfway through.

5. To cook the orecchiette, place in a large pot of boiling, salted water until they are tender but still chewy, 3 to 4 minutes.

YIELD: **1 LB.**

ACTIVE TIME: **30 MINUTES**

TOTAL TIME: **2 HOURS AND 15 MINUTES**

Pizzoccheri

INGREDIENTS

1 CUP BUCKWHEAT FLOUR

1 CUP ALL-PURPOSE FLOUR

½ TEASPOON SALT, PLUS MORE
TO TASTE

¼ CUP VERY WARM WATER (160°F),
PLUS MORE AS NEEDED

2 LARGE EGGS

SEMOLINA FLOUR, AS NEEDED

DIRECTIONS

1. In a mixing bowl or on a work surface, combine the flours and salt and form the mixture into a mound. Create a well in the center and place the water and eggs in the well. Using a fork or your fingers, gradually start incorporating the flour into the well until the dough starts holding together in a single mass. Incorporate more water, 1 tablespoon at a time, if the mixture is too dry to hold together. Once the dough feels firm and dry and can be formed into a ball, it's time to start kneading.

2. Work any remaining flour into the ball of dough. Using the heel of your hand, push the ball of dough away from you. Turn the dough 45 degrees each time you repeat this motion, as doing so incorporates the flour more evenly. As you continue to knead, you'll notice the dough getting less and less floury. Eventually it will have a smooth, elastic texture. If the dough still feels wet or tacky, dust it with flour and continue kneading. If it feels too dry and is not completely sticking together, wet your hands with water and continue kneading. Wet your hands as many times as you need to until the dough is smooth and springy, about 8 to 10 minutes. The dough has been sufficiently kneaded when it gently pulls back when stretched.

3. Wrap the ball of dough tightly in plastic wrap and let it rest for 40 minutes hours at room temperature. The dough will keep for up to 3 days in the refrigerator, but may experience some discoloration.

Continued...

4. Cut the dough into four even pieces. Set one piece on a smooth work surface and cover the rest in plastic wrap to prevent them from drying out. Shape the piece of dough into a ball, place it on the surface, and, with the palm of your hand, push down on it so that it looks like a thick pita. Using a rolling pin, roll the dough to ½ inch thick. Try as much as possible to keep the thickness and width of the dough even, as it will help the dough fit through the pasta maker more easily.

5. Lightly dust the piece of dough with semolina flour and, using a rolling pin, roll it until it is approximately 4 inches wide and 8 inches long. Run the dough three times through the widest setting of the pasta maker. The dough will now be 12 to 15 inches long and 4 to 5 inches wide. Repeat this process with the remaining pieces of dough. Hang the pieces of dough across a wooden drying rack and let them dry for 30 minutes, turning the sheets over twice during that time.

6. Lightly dust one sheet of dough with semolina flour and gently roll it up. Gently slice the roll across into ⅓-inch wide ribbons, taking care not to compress the roll too much as you slice through it. Repeat with the remaining pieces of dough. Lightly dust the pasta with semolina flour, then unroll them and place them on parchment-lined baking sheets. Let them rest for 30 minutes before cooking.

YIELD: **1 LB.**

ACTIVE TIME: **45 MINUTES**

TOTAL TIME: **4 HOURS**

Fazzoletti

INGREDIENTS

BASIC PASTA DOUGH (SEE PAGE 20)

SEMOLINA FLOUR, AS NEEDED

SALT, TO TASTE

DIRECTIONS

1. Prepare the dough as directed, rolling the dough to the thinnest setting (generally notch 5) for pasta sheets that are about 1⁄16 inch thick. Lay the pasta sheets on flour-dusted, parchment-lined baking sheets and let them dry for 15 minutes.

2. Cut each pasta sheet into as many 2½-inch squares as possible. Set them on flour-dusted, parchment-lined baking sheets so they are not touching. Gather any scraps into a ball, put it through the pasta maker to create additional pasta sheets, and cut those as well. Allow them to dry for 1 hour, turning them over once halfway through, and then cook. Alternatively, you can place them, once dried, in a bowl, cover with a kitchen towel, and refrigerate for up to 3 days.

3. To cook the fazzoletti, cook for about 1 minute in a pot of boiling, salted water, until they are tender but still chewy.

YIELD: **1½ LBS.**

ACTIVE TIME: **1 HOUR**

TOTAL TIME: **4 HOURS**

Garganelli

INGREDIENTS

2¼ CUPS SEMOLINA FLOUR, PLUS MORE AS NEEDED

1½ TEASPOONS SALT, PLUS MORE TO TASTE

3 LARGE EGGS

2 TABLESPOONS OLIVE OIL

2 TABLESPOONS WATER

DIRECTIONS

1. In a mixing bowl or on a work surface, combine the flour and salt and form it into a mound. Create a well in the center and place the eggs, olive oil, and the water in the well. Using a fork or your fingers, gradually start incorporating the flour into the well until the dough starts holding together in a single mass. Incorporate more water, 1 tablespoon at a time, if the mixture is too dry to hold together. Once the dough feels firm and dry and can be formed into a ball, it's time to start kneading.

2. Work any remaining flour into the ball of dough. Using the heel of your hand, push the ball of dough away from you. Turn the dough 45 degrees each time you repeat this motion, as doing so incorporates the flour more evenly. As you continue to knead, you'll notice the dough getting less and less floury. Eventually it will have a smooth, elastic texture. If the dough still feels wet or tacky, dust it with flour and continue kneading. If it feels too dry and is not completely sticking together, wet your hands with water and continue kneading. Wet your hands as many times as you need to until the dough is smooth and springy, about 8 to 10 minutes. The dough has been sufficiently kneaded when it gently pulls back when stretched.

3. Wrap the ball of dough tightly in plastic wrap and let it rest for 2 hours at room temperature. The dough will keep for up to 3 days in the refrigerator, but may experience some discoloration.

Continued...

4. Cut the dough into four even pieces. Set one piece on a smooth work surface and cover the rest in plastic wrap to prevent them from drying out. Shape the piece of dough into a ball, place it on the surface, and, with the palm of your hand, push down on it so that it looks like a thick pita. Using a rolling pin, roll the dough to ½ inch thick. Try as much as possible to keep the thickness and width of the dough even, as it will make it easier to run the dough through the pasta maker.

5. Run the dough through the pasta maker, rolling the dough to the second-thinnest setting (generally notch 4) for pasta sheets that are about ⅛ inch thick. Lay the pasta sheets on flour-dusted, parchment-lined baking sheets and cover them loosely with plastic wrap.

6. Working with one sheet at a time, lightly dust it with flour. Cut it into 1½-inch-wide strips and then cut the strips into 1½-inch squares. Repeat with the remaining pasta sheets. Cover the squares loosely with plastic wrap. Gather any scraps together into a ball, put it through the pasta maker to create additional pasta sheets, and cut those in the same fashion.

7. To make each garganello, place one square of pasta dough on a flour-dusted work surface with one of the corners pointing toward you. Using a chopstick, gently roll the square of pasta around the chopstick, starting from the corner closest to you, until a tube forms. Once completely rolled, press down slightly as you seal the ends together, then carefully slide the tube of pasta off the chopstick and lightly dust it with flour. Set them on flour-dusted, parchment-lined baking sheets and allow them to dry for 1 hour, turning them over halfway through.

8. To cook the garganelli, cook for 2 to 3 minutes in a pot of boiling, salted water, until they are tender but still chewy.

YIELD: **1 LB.**

ACTIVE TIME: **45 MINUTES**

TOTAL TIME: **5 HOURS**

Nodi

INGREDIENTS

1¾ CUPS SEMOLINA FLOUR, PLUS
MORE AS NEEDED

1 TEASPOON SALT, PLUS MORE
TO TASTE

½ TEASPOON FENNEL SEEDS,
GROUND FINE

⅔ CUP WARM WATER (105°F)

DIRECTIONS

1. Place the flour, salt, and fennel seeds in a large bowl and add the water. Work the mixture with a fork until it starts to stick together and look coarse. Transfer it to a flour-dusted work surface.

2. Using the heel of your hand, push the ball of dough away from you. Turn the dough 45 degrees each time you repeat this motion, as doing so incorporates the flour more evenly. As you continue to knead, you'll notice the dough getting less and less floury. Eventually it will have a smooth, elastic texture. If the dough still feels wet or tacky, dust it with flour and continue kneading. If it feels too dry and is not completely sticking together, wet your hands with water and continue kneading. Wet your hands as many times as you need to until the dough is smooth and springy, about 8 to 10 minutes. The dough has been sufficiently kneaded when it gently pulls back when stretched.

3. Wrap the ball of dough tightly in plastic wrap and let it rest for 2 hours at room temperature. The dough will keep for up to 3 days in the refrigerator, but may experience some discoloration.

4. Place the dough on a flour-dusted work surface, roll it into a 2-inch-thick log and cut it into 18 rounds. Cover all the pieces but the one you are working on with plastic wrap to keep them from drying out.

    Continued...

5. Roll each piece of dough into a long rope that is ⅛ inch thick. Starting at one end of the rope, tie a simple knot, gently pull on both ends to tighten the knot slightly, then cut the knot off the rope, leaving a tail on each side that is about ⅜ inch long. Keep making and cutting off knots in this manner until you use up all of the rope. Repeat with the remaining pieces of dough. Set the finished knots on flour-dusted, parchment-lined baking sheets, making sure they are not touching. Allow them to dry for 2 hours, turning them over once halfway through.

6. To cook the nodi, place in a large pot of boiling, salted water for 2 to 3 minutes, until they are tender but still firm.

Tajarin

INGREDIENTS

ALL-YOLK PASTA DOUGH (PAGE 22)

SEMOLINA FLOUR, AS NEEDED

SALT, TO TASTE

DIRECTIONS

1. Prepare the dough as directed, rolling the dough to the thinnest setting (generally notch 5) for pasta sheets that are about ⅟₁₆ inch thick. Cut the pieces into 8-inch-long sheets, lay them on flour-dusted, parchment-lined baking sheets, and let them dry for 15 minutes.

2. Working with one sheet at a time, dust it with semolina flour and gently roll it up. Using a very sharp knife, gently slice the roll into ½-inch-wide strips. Dust the strips with flour, then gently unfold the strips, one at a time, shaking off any excess flour. Arrange them on flour-dusted, parchment-lined baking sheets, either straight and spread out or curled into a coil. Repeat with all the pasta sheets. Allow the tajarin to dry for 30 minutes before cooking.

3. To cook the tajarin, cook in a large pot of boiling, salted water until they are tender but still chewy, typically no more than 2 minutes.

YIELD: **1 LB.**

ACTIVE TIME: **45 MINUTES**

TOTAL TIME: **5 HOURS**

Trofie

INGREDIENTS

2¾ CUPS ALL-PURPOSE FLOUR

1 TEASPOON SALT, PLUS MORE
TO TASTE

1 CUP WATER

SEMOLINA FLOUR, AS NEEDED

DIRECTIONS

1. Place the flour and salt in a large bowl, stir to combine, and add the water. Work the mixture with a fork until all the water has been incorporated. Work the mixture with your hands until a coarse dough forms.

2. Transfer the dough, along with any bits that stuck to the bowl, to a flour-dusted work surface and knead the dough. Using the heel of your hand, push the ball of dough away from you in a downward motion. Turn the dough 45 degrees each time you repeat this motion, as doing so incorporates the flour more evenly. Knead the dough until it is smooth and elastic, about 10 minutes. Cover the dough with plastic wrap and let it rest at room temperature for 2 hours.

3. Place the dough on a flour-dusted work surface and roll it into a 2-inch-thick log. Cut it into eight pieces, leave one out, and cover the rest with plastic wrap. Shape each piece of dough into a ball, roll it out until it is a long, ½-inch-thick rope. Cut it into ½-inch pieces and dust them with flour. Working with one piece at a time, press down on the dough with your fingertips and roll it down the palm of your other hand. This will cause the piece of dough to turn into a narrow spiral with tapered ends. Repeat with the remaining pieces of dough. Dust the spirals with flour, place them on flour-dusted, parchment-lined baking sheets, and allow them to dry for 2 hours, turning them over halfway through.

4. To cook the trofie, place in a large pot of boiling, salted water until they are tender but still chewy, 3 to 4 minutes.

Gnocchi

INGREDIENTS

3 LBS. YUKON GOLD POTATOES

2 LARGE EGGS

2½ CUPS ALL-PURPOSE FLOUR, PLUS MORE AS NEEDED

1 TABLESPOON SALT, PLUS MORE TO TASTE

DIRECTIONS

1. Preheat the oven to 400°F. Place the potatoes on a baking sheet, prick them several times with a fork, and bake until they are soft all the way through, about 1 hour. Remove from oven, slice them open, and let cool completely.

2. When the potatoes are cool enough to handle, scoop the flesh into a mixing bowl and mash until smooth. Make a well in the center of the potatoes and add the eggs, 1½ cups of the flour, and the salt. Work the mixture with your hands to combine, and then add the remaining flour in small increments. Knead the dough to incorporate and stop adding flour as soon as the dough holds together and is no longer tacky.

3. Place a handful of dough on a flour-dusted work surface and roll it into a ¾-inch-thick rope. Repeat with the remaining dough. Cut the ropes into ½-inch-wide pieces and roll the gnocchi over the tines of a fork, or a gnocchi board, while gently pressing down to create ridges. If the gnocchi start sticking to the fork, dip it into flour before pressing the gnocchi against it. Place the shaped gnocchi on a parchment-lined baking sheet and dust them with flour.

4. To cook the gnocchi, bring a large pot of water to a boil. Working in small batches, add salt and the gnocchi and stir to keep the gnocchi from sticking to the bottom. The gnocchi will eventually float to the surface. Cook for 1 more minute, remove, and transfer to a parchment-lined baking sheet to cool.

TIP: Sautéing gnocchi in butter or olive oil after boiling them adds a nice bit of flavor.

Sweet Potato Gnocchi

INGREDIENTS

2½ LBS. SWEET POTATOES

½ CUP RICOTTA CHEESE

1 EGG

2 EGG YOLKS

1 TABLESPOON KOSHER SALT, PLUS MORE TO TASTE

1 TEASPOON BLACK PEPPER

3 TABLESPOONS LIGHT BROWN SUGAR

2 TABLESPOONS REAL MAPLE SYRUP

2 CUPS ALL-PURPOSE FLOUR, PLUS MORE AS NEEDED

1 CUP SEMOLINA FLOUR

2 TABLESPOONS OLIVE OIL

DIRECTIONS

1. Preheat the oven to 350°F. Wash the sweet potatoes, place them on a parchment-lined baking sheet, and use a knife to poke several holes in the tops of the potatoes. Place in the oven and cook until they are soft all the way through, 45 minutes to 1 hour. Remove from the oven, slice them open, and let cool completely.

2. Scrape the cooled sweet potato flesh into a mixing bowl and mash until smooth. Add the ricotta, egg, egg yolks, salt, pepper, brown sugar, and maple syrup and stir until thoroughly combined. Add the flours 1 cup at a time and work the mixture with your hands until incorporated. The dough should not feel tacky when touched. If it is tacky, incorporate more all-purpose flour, 1 teaspoon at a time, until it has the right texture. Coat a mixing bowl with the olive oil and set it aside.

3. Transfer the dough to a lightly floured work surface and cut it into 10 even pieces. Roll each piece into a long rope and cut the ropes into ¾-inch-wide pieces. Roll the gnocchi over a fork, or a gnocchi board, pressing down gently to form them into the desired shapes. Place the formed gnocchi on a parchment-lined, flour-dusted baking sheet.

4. To cook the gnocchi, bring a large pot of water to a boil. Add salt once the water is boiling. Working in small batches, add the gnocchi and stir to keep them from sticking to the bottom. The gnocchi will eventually float to the surface. Cook for 1 more minute, remove, and transfer to the bowl containing the olive oil. Toss to coat and place on a parchment-lined baking sheet to cool.

Chickpea Gnocchetti

INGREDIENTS

1 (14 OZ.) CAN OF CHICKPEAS, DRAINED AND RINSED

4 LARGE EGG YOLKS

1 TABLESPOON WATER

1½ CUPS ALL-PURPOSE FLOUR, PLUS MORE AS NEEDED

1½ TEASPOONS SALT, PLUS MORE TO TASTE

DIRECTIONS

1. Remove the outer skin from each chickpea. Place the chickpeas, egg yolks, and water in a food processor and puree until smooth. Transfer the puree to a mixing bowl and add the flour and salt. Knead until a soft, tacky dough forms, about 8 minutes. The dough should have no elasticity whatsoever. If you poke it with a finger, the indentation should remain.

2. Dust a work surface with flour. Tear off a handful of the dough and cover the remainder with plastic wrap to keep it from drying out. Roll the dough into a long rope that is about ½ inch thick and cut the ropes into ½-inch-wide pieces. Roll the gnocchetti over the tines of a fork, or a gnocchi board, while gently pressing down to create ridges. If the gnocchetti start sticking to the fork, dip it into flour before pressing the gnocchetti against it. Place the shaped dumplings on a parchment-lined baking sheet and dust them with flour.

3. To cook the gnocchetti, bring a large pot of water to a boil. Working in small batches, add salt and the gnocchetti and stir to keep them from sticking to the bottom. The gnocchetti will eventually float to the surface. Cook for 1 more minute, remove, and transfer to a parchment-lined baking sheet to cool.

YIELD: **1 LB.**

ACTIVE TIME: **20 MINUTES**

TOTAL TIME: **2 HOURS AND 30 MINUTES**

Passatelli

INGREDIENTS

1¼ CUPS VERY FINE BREAD CRUMBS

1¼ CUPS GRATED PARMESAN CHEESE

2 TABLESPOONS UNSALTED BUTTER, MELTED

1 HANDFUL OF FRESH PARSLEY LEAVES, FINELY CHOPPED

3 LARGE EGGS, PLUS MORE AS NEEDED

1 TEASPOON FRESHLY GRATED NUTMEG OR LEMON ZEST

1 TEASPOON SALT, PLUS MORE TO TASTE

½ TEASPOON WHITE PEPPER

DIRECTIONS

1. Place the bread crumbs, Parmesan, butter, parsley, eggs, nutmeg or lemon zest, salt, and pepper in a large mixing bowl. Work the mixture with your hands until a firm, slightly tacky dough forms. If the mixture feels too wet, incorporate more bread crumbs, 1 tablespoon at a time. Cover the dough with plastic wrap and let it rest at room temperature for 15 minutes.

2. Bring water to a boil in a small saucepan. Form a pinch of dough into a ball and drop it in the water. If it falls apart, add another egg to the dough and stir to incorporate. Working in batches, place handfuls of dough into the cup of a spätzle maker that has been oiled with nonstick cooking spray. Press down to squeeze long ropes of dough out the other side. Cut the ropes into 1½-inch-long pieces and transfer them to a parchment-lined baking sheet. Let dry for 1½ hours.

3. To cook the passatelli, bring a large pot of water to a boil. Reduce the heat so that the water comes to a gentle boil and add salt and the passatelli. After they float to the surface, about 4 minutes, let them cook for a minute longer.

NOTE: Spätzle makers are very reasonably priced, about $7 for a serviceable one. If you do not have one, you can use a box grater to form the long ropes.

YIELD: **1 LB.**

ACTIVE TIME: **30 MINUTES**

TOTAL TIME: **1 HOUR AND 30 MINUTES**

Spätzle

INGREDIENTS

2½ CUPS ALL-PURPOSE FLOUR

1 TABLESPOON SALT, PLUS MORE TO TASTE

2 LARGE EGGS

1¼ CUPS WHOLE MILK, PLUS MORE AS NEEDED

DIRECTIONS

1. Place the flour, salt, eggs, and milk in a mixing bowl and stir until the dough becomes somewhat shiny and resembles pancake batter, 7 to 8 minutes. If the dough seems too thick, incorporate more milk, 1 teaspoon at a time. Cover the bowl with plastic wrap and let rest at room temperature for 1 hour.

2. Bring a large pot of water to a boil and prepare an ice water bath. Reduce the heat so the water is gently boiling and add salt. Working in batches, place handfuls of dough into the cup of a spätzle maker that has been oiled with nonstick cooking spray. While pressing down, grate the dough into the boiling water and cook until the spätzle floats to the top, stirring occasionally to prevent the spätzle from sticking to the bottom. Remove the cooked spätzle with a slotted spoon and transfer them to the ice water bath. When all of the spätzle are cooked, place them on paper towels to dry.

TIP: Spätzle, much like gnocchi, are wonderful after being sautéed in butter or olive oil.

YIELD: **1¼ LBS.**

ACTIVE TIME: **45 MINUTES**

TOTAL TIME: **2 HOURS**

Sweet Potato Spätzle

INGREDIENTS

3 LBS. SWEET POTATOES

1 CUP ALL-PURPOSE FLOUR

1 TEASPOON SALT, PLUS MORE
TO TASTE

2 EGGS, SEPARATED INTO YOLKS
AND WHITES

DIRECTIONS

1. Preheat the oven to 400°F. Place the sweet potatoes on a baking sheet, prick them several times with a fork, and bake until they are soft all the way through, 45 minutes to 1 hour. Remove from oven, slice them open, and let cool completely.

2. When the sweet potatoes are cool enough to handle, scoop the flesh into the work bowl of a food processor and puree until smooth. Place the sweet potato puree in a saucepan and cook, stirring frequently, over low heat until the puree has reduced to 2 cups, about 30 minutes. This will help concentrate the flavor. Transfer the reduced puree to a mixing bowl and let cool for 10 minutes.

3. Bring a pot of water to a boil and prepare an ice water bath. Add the flour and salt to the puree and fold to incorporate. Add the egg yolks and whisk to combine. Place the egg whites in a separate bowl and beat until soft peaks form. Fold the beaten egg whites into the sweet potato mixture.

4. Reduce the heat so the water is gently boiling and add salt. Working in batches, place handfuls of dough into the cup of a spätzle maker that has been oiled with nonstick cooking spray. While pressing down, grate the dough into the boiling water and cook until the spätzle floats to the top, stirring occasionally to prevent the spätzle from sticking to the bottom. Remove the cooked spätzle with a slotted spoon and transfer them to the ice water bath. When all of the spätzle are cooked, place them on paper towels to dry.

TIP: The sweet potato can be replaced by pumpkin, or any other member of the squash family.

YIELD: **1 LB.**

ACTIVE TIME: **1 HOUR**

TOTAL TIME: **2 HOURS**

Chard Spätzle

INGREDIENTS

1½ TABLESPOONS SALT, PLUS
MORE TO TASTE

2 LBS. SWISS CHARD, STEMS
REMOVED

4 LARGE EGGS

1 TEASPOON FRESHLY GRATED
NUTMEG

2 CUPS ALL-PURPOSE FLOUR,
PLUS MORE AS NEEDED

¼ CUP WATER

MILK, AT ROOM TEMPERATURE,
AS NEEDED

BUTTER OR OLIVE OIL, AS NEEDED

DIRECTIONS

1. Bring a large pot of water to a boil. Add salt and the chard and cook until the chard has wilted, about 3 minutes. Drain the chard and rinse under cold water. Drain well and squeeze to remove as much liquid as possible. Transfer to a clean kitchen towel and pat the leaves dry.

2. Place the chard, eggs, nutmeg, and 1½ tablespoons salt in a food processor and pulse until the greens are mostly shredded. Add the flour and water and blitz until the mixture is smooth, stopping to scrape down the work bowl as needed. Transfer the dough to a mixing bowl. The dough should resemble pancake batter. If it seems too thick, incorporate milk, 1 teaspoon at a time. Cover the dough with plastic wrap and let sit for 1 hour.

3. Bring a large pot of water to a boil and prepare an ice water bath. Add salt and reduce the heat so that the water is gently boiling. Working in batches, place handfuls of dough into the cup of a spätzle maker that has been oiled with nonstick cooking spray. While pressing down, grate the dough into the boiling water and cook until the spätzle floats to the top. Stir occasionally to prevent the spätzle from sticking to the bottom. Remove the cooked spätzle with a slotted spoon and transfer them to the ice water bath. When all of the spätzle are cooked, place them on paper towels to dry. Sauté in butter or olive oil and serve.

YIELD: **1 LB.**

ACTIVE TIME: **30 MINUTES**

TOTAL TIME: **2 HOURS AND 45 MINUTES**

Pizzicotti

INGREDIENTS

4 CUPS ALL-PURPOSE FLOUR

2½ TEASPOONS ACTIVE DRY YEAST

2 TEASPOONS SALT, PLUS MORE
TO TASTE

1¼ CUPS WARM WATER (105°F)

SEMOLINA FLOUR, AS NEEDED

DIRECTIONS

1. Place the all-purpose flour, yeast, and salt in a large
    bowl and stir to combine. Gradually incorporate the
    water and work the mixture with a fork until it starts
    holding together. Work the dough with your hands
    until it feels firm and dry. Transfer the dough to a flour-
    dusted work surface and knead it until it is very smooth
    and gently pulls back into place when stretched, 8 to 10
    minutes. Place the dough in a large bowl, cover it with
    plastic wrap, and let it rise in a naturally warm place
    until it doubles in size, about 1 hour.

2. Remove the dough from the bowl and knead it just
    enough to remove any air trapped inside. Place the
    dough on a parchment-lined baking sheet, cover it with
    a kitchen towel, and let it rise for another hour in
    a naturally warm place.

3. Bring a large pot of water to a boil. Add salt to the
    water once it is boiling. Knead the dough to remove
    any air, pinch off peanut-sized pieces of the dough,
    and drop them in the boiling water, working in batches
    if necessary. Cook until they float to the surface, 2 to
    3 minutes, and drain.

    *TIP: Pizzicotti are wonderful with rich, thick sauces, such as the
    Lamb Ragù on page 84.*

Tarhana

INGREDIENTS

3 VERY RIPE PLUM TOMATOES

1 RED BELL PEPPER, STEMMED, SEEDS AND RIBS REMOVED, AND MINCED

1 LARGE ONION, CHOPPED

¾ TABLESPOON DRIED THYME

SALT AND PEPPER, TO TASTE

2 CUPS SEMOLINA FLOUR, PLUS MORE AS NEEDED

½ CUP FULL-FAT PLAIN GREEK YOGURT

1¾ CUPS BREAD FLOUR, PLUS 1½ TEASPOONS

DIRECTIONS

1. Bring a water to a boil in a medium saucepan. Add the tomatoes and parboil for 1 minute. Use tongs to transfer them to a cutting board and let them cool. When the tomatoes are cool enough to handle, peel the tomatoes, cut them into quarters, remove the seeds, and chop the remaining flesh.

2. Warm a large skillet over medium-low heat for 2 to 3 minutes. Raise the heat to medium, add the tomatoes, bell pepper, onion, and thyme, season with salt and pepper, and stir to combine. Bring the mixture to a boil, reduce the heat to low, cover the pan, and cook for 40 minutes, stirring occasionally, until the mixture resembles a watery, chunky tomato sauce. Remove the pan from heat and let the mixture cool.

3. Place the mixture in a food processor and blitz until pureed. Strain through a fine sieve into a bowl, add the semolina flour and a generous pinch of salt, and stir to combine. Cover the bowl with plastic wrap and let it rest at room temperature for 1 hour.

4. Line two rimmed baking sheets with parchment paper. Preheat the oven to 200°F and position a rack in the center. Stir the yogurt into the semolina mixture, add the bread flour, and stir until the mixture holds together as a dough. Transfer the dough to a flour-dusted work surface, dust the dough with flour, and begin kneading it. Using the heel of your hand, push the dough away from you in a downward motion. Turn the dough 45 degrees each time you repeat this motion, as doing so incorporates the flour more evenly. Knead until the dough has a smooth, elastic texture, 8 to 10 minutes.

Continued...

5. Divide the dough into three pieces, patting each one into a ¼-inch-thick round. Place the rounds on the prepared baking sheets and place them in the oven. Lower the oven's temperature to 175°F and bake for 1 hour. Flip the rounds over, return them to the oven, and bake for another hour. Remove from the oven and leave it at 175°F. The rounds should be quite firm but not rock hard. Let the rounds cool completely.

6. Break each round in half and, using the large holes on a box grater, grate them into large crumbs. Spread the crumbs on the baking sheets, place in the oven, and bake until they are rock hard, which will take about 1½ hours. Remove from the oven and let cool completely.

7. To cook tarhana, place it in a large pot of boiling, salted water, reduce the heat to low, and simmer until tender but chewy, about 20 minutes.

CHAPTER 2

SAUCES

Yes, a classic Marinara Sauce (see page 67) is tough to beat, but sticking to just that fails to get the most out of your pasta. A large part of why it has become a global sensation is the innumerable flavors it can accommodate, as you'll see from the tempting array presented in this chapter.

The sauces here are only a smattering of what's available out there, but we're betting the variety is wide enough to keep your beloved pastas from growing stale, and present the picky eaters in your life something new in an easy-to-accept package.

Marinara Sauce

INGREDIENTS

4 LBS. TOMATOES, PEELED, SEEDED, AND CHOPPED

1 YELLOW ONION, SLICED

15 GARLIC CLOVES, CRUSHED

2 TEASPOONS FINELY CHOPPED FRESH THYME

2 TEASPOONS FINELY CHOPPED FRESH OREGANO

2 TABLESPOONS OLIVE OIL

1½ TABLESPOONS KOSHER SALT, PLUS MORE TO TASTE

1 TEASPOON BLACK PEPPER, PLUS MORE TO TASTE

2 TABLESPOONS FINELY CHOPPED FRESH BASIL

1 TABLESPOON FINELY CHOPPED FRESH PARSLEY

DIRECTIONS

1. Place all of the ingredients, except for the basil and parsley, in a large saucepan and cook, stirring constantly, over medium heat until the tomatoes begin to collapse, about 10 minutes.

2. Reduce the heat to low and cook, stirring occasionally, for about 1½ hours, or until the flavor is to your liking.

3. Stir in the basil and parsley and season the sauce to taste. The sauce will be chunky. If you prefer a smoother texture, transfer the sauce to a food processor and blitz before serving with your pasta.

YIELD: **3 CUPS**

ACTIVE TIME: **10 MINUTES**

TOTAL TIME: **25 MINUTES**

Arrabbiata Sauce

INGREDIENTS

2 TABLESPOONS OLIVE OIL

3 GARLIC CLOVES, CRUSHED

2 DRIED CHILI PEPPERS, SEEDED
AND CHOPPED

1 (28 OZ.) CAN OF PEELED WHOLE
SAN MARZANO TOMATOES, WITH
THEIR LIQUID

1 HANDFUL OF FRESH PARSLEY,
CHOPPED

SALT AND PEPPER, TO TASTE

DIRECTIONS

1. Warm a large, deep skillet over low heat for 1 to 2
    minutes. Add the olive oil, garlic, and chilies, raise the
    heat to medium-low, and cook until the garlic begins to
    brown, about 1 minute. Remove the garlic and as much
    of the chili peppers as possible and add the tomatoes,
    breaking them up with your hands as you add them to
    the pan. Add the liquid from the can, raise the heat to
    medium-high, and bring to a boil. Reduce the heat to
    medium-low and cook, while stirring occasionally, until
    the sauce is thick and the oil has risen to the surface,
    about 20 minutes.

2. Stir in the parsley, season with salt and pepper, and serve
    with your favorite pasta.

YIELD: **2 CUPS**

ACTIVE TIME: **15 MINUTES**

TOTAL TIME: **25 MINUTES**

Basil Pesto

INGREDIENTS

¼ CUP PINE NUTS

2 GARLIC CLOVES

SALT AND PEPPER, TO TASTE

2 CUPS TIGHTLY PACKED FRESH BASIL LEAVES

½ CUP OLIVE OIL

¼ CUP GRATED PECORINO ROMANO CHEESE

¼ CUP GRATED PARMESAN CHEESE

DIRECTIONS

1. Warm a small skillet over low heat for 1 minute. Add the pine nuts and cook, while shaking the pan, until they become a light golden brown, about 2 minutes. Transfer to a plate and let cool.

2. Place the pine nuts, garlic, salt, and pepper in a food processor and pulse until ground. Add the basil and pulse until finely minced. Transfer the mixture to a medium bowl and add the oil in a thin stream as you whisk it in.

3. Stir in the cheeses and serve.

TIP: Substituting toasted hazelnuts and Manchego cheese will inject even more nuttiness into your pesto.

YIELD: **8 CUPS**

ACTIVE TIME: **15 MINUTES**

TOTAL TIME: **30 MINUTES**

Rose Sauce

INGREDIENTS

4 LBS. VERY RIPE PLUM TOMATOES, PEELED, SEEDED, AND CHOPPED

4 TABLESPOONS UNSALTED BUTTER

½ WHITE OR VIDALIA ONION, QUARTERED

SALT AND PEPPER, TO TASTE

1 TEASPOON SUGAR (OPTIONAL)

2 CUPS HEAVY CREAM

DIRECTIONS

1. Place the tomatoes in a food processor and blitz until pureed.

2. Warm a medium saucepan over medium-low heat for 2 minutes. Add the butter and raise the heat to medium. Once the butter melts and stops foaming, add the onion and a pinch of salt and sauté until it begins to sizzle. Reduce the heat to low, cover the pan, and cook the onion, stirring occasionally, until the onion is soft, about 10 minutes.

3. Add the pureed tomatoes and a few pinches of salt. If the tomatoes are not in season, stir in the sugar. Bring to a boil, reduce the heat to low, and simmer until the sauce has thickened and the flavor is to your liking, about 20 minutes. Remove as much of the onion as you can with a slotted spoon.

4. As the tomato sauce cooks, place the cream in a small saucepan and cook over low heat until it has reduced by about half. Remove the pan from heat and set the cream aside.

5. Stir the reduced cream into the tomato sauce, season it with salt and pepper, and serve.

Fontina Sauce

INGREDIENTS

FLORETS FROM 1 HEAD OF
CAULIFLOWER

6 TABLESPOONS OLIVE OIL

SALT AND PEPPER, TO TASTE

1 LB. CREMINI MUSHROOMS,
STEMMED AND CHOPPED

3 TABLESPOONS FINELY CHOPPED
FRESH THYME

6 OZ. BACON, CHOPPED

1 LARGE YELLOW ONION, GRATED

½ CUP CHICKEN STOCK
(SEE PAGE 109)

1 CUP GRATED FONTINA CHEESE

¾ CUP HEAVY CREAM

1½ TEASPOONS WORCESTERSHIRE
SAUCE

DIRECTIONS

1. Preheat the oven to 450°F. Place the cauliflower and 2 tablespoons of the olive oil in a large bowl and toss to coat. Transfer the cauliflower to a baking pan, season it with salt and pepper, cover the pan with foil, and then place in the oven. Cook for 15 minutes, remove from the oven, remove the foil, and turn the cauliflower over. Return the pan to the oven, uncovered, lower the oven's temperature to 400°F, and roast the cauliflower until it is tender and the edges are browned, about 40 minutes.

2. While the cauliflower is roasting, place the mushrooms in a large bowl with 2 tablespoons of the olive oil and toss to coat. Transfer to a parchment-lined baking sheet, season with salt and pepper, and sprinkle the thyme over the top. Place in the 400°F oven, roast for 15 minutes, and remove from oven. Carefully drain the liquid, return to the oven, and roast until the mushrooms are soft and lightly browned, about 25 minutes.

3. Warm a large skillet over medium-low heat for 2 minutes. Add 2 tablespoons of the olive oil and raise the heat to medium. When the oil starts to shimmer, add the bacon and sauté until it is browned and crisp, about 8 minutes. Transfer it to a small bowl and set aside.

4. Add the onion to the pan, season it with salt, and raise the heat to medium-high. Sauté until the onion starts to sizzle. Reduce the heat to low, cover the pan, and cook, while stirring occasionally, until the onion becomes very soft, about 15 minutes. Raise the heat to medium-high, stir in the stock, cheese, and cream, and cook until the mixture starts to bubble. Stir in the Worcestershire sauce, serve with pasta, and top with the bacon and roasted vegetables.

Calamari Fra Diavolo

INGREDIENTS

1 CUP DRY RED WINE

2 LBS. SQUID, BODIES CUT
INTO RINGS, TENTACLES HALVED
LENGTHWISE

3 TABLESPOONS OLIVE OIL

4 GARLIC CLOVES, MINCED

1 TEASPOON RED PEPPER FLAKES

SALT, TO TASTE

3 ANCHOVY FILLETS IN OLIVE OIL

1 HANDFUL OF FRESH PARSLEY,
CHOPPED

1 (28 OZ.) CAN OF PEELED WHOLE
PLUM TOMATOES, PUREED

½ CUP CLAM JUICE

DIRECTIONS

1. Place the wine in a small saucepan, bring it to a boil, and cook until it has reduced by half, about 5 minutes. Remove the pan from heat and set it aside.

2. Rinse the squid thoroughly and transfer it to a paper towel–lined plate. Pat the squid with paper towels to remove as much surface moisture as possible.

3. Place the olive oil in a large, deep skillet and warm over medium heat for 2 to 3 minutes. When the oil starts to shimmer, add the garlic, half of the red pepper flakes, and a pinch of salt and sauté until the garlic starts to brown, about 1 minute. Raise the heat to medium-high and add the squid, anchovies, and parsley. Cook, while occasionally, until the anchovies dissolve and the squid is golden brown, about 5 minutes.

4. Add the reduced wine and continue to cook until the liquid in the mixture has reduced by one-third, about 5 minutes. Stir in the tomatoes, the clam juice, and remaining red pepper flakes, season with salt, bring to a boil, and then reduce the heat to medium-low. Simmer until the sauce has thickened slightly, about 20 minutes, and serve with pasta.

Aromatic Walnut Sauce

YIELD: **2 CUPS**

ACTIVE TIME: **20 MINUTES**

TOTAL TIME: **50 MINUTES**

INGREDIENTS

1 CUP DAY-OLD BREAD PIECES

1 CUP WALNUTS

1 GARLIC CLOVE, SLICED THIN

¼ CUP BREAD CRUMBS

1 HANDFUL OF FRESH PARSLEY, CHOPPED

2 TABLESPOONS FINELY CHOPPED FRESH MARJORAM

3 TABLESPOONS WALNUT OIL

3 TABLESPOONS HEAVY CREAM

5 TABLESPOONS UNSALTED BUTTER, AT ROOM TEMPERATURE

SALT, TO TASTE

DIRECTIONS

1. Place the bread in a small bowl, cover it with warm water, and let it soak for 30 minutes. Drain, squeeze the bread to remove as much water from it as possible, and set it aside.

2. Bring a small saucepan of water to a boil, add the walnuts, cook for 2 minutes, drain, and let them cool. When cool enough to handle, rub off their skins and place on paper towels to dry. When dry, chop the walnuts and transfer them to a small bowl.

3. Place the bread, walnuts, garlic, bread crumbs, parsley, and half of the marjoram in a food processor and pulse until the mixture is a smooth paste. Transfer to a bowl, stir in the walnut oil until it has been thoroughly incorporated, and then stir in the cream and the butter. Season with salt and warm in a saucepan before serving over pasta.

Puttanesca Sauce

INGREDIENTS

½ CUP OLIVE OIL

3 GARLIC CLOVES, MINCED

1 (28 OZ.) CAN OF PEELED
WHOLE SAN MARZANO TOMATOES,
CRUSHED BY HAND AND WITH
THEIR LIQUID

½ LB. BLACK OLIVES, PITTED

¼ CUP NONPAREIL CAPERS

5 ANCHOVY FILLETS IN OLIVE OIL

1 TEASPOON RED PEPPER FLAKES

SALT AND PEPPER, TO TASTE

DIRECTIONS

1. Place the olive oil in a large, deep skillet and warm over medium heat. When the oil begins to shimmer, add the garlic and sauté until fragrant, about 1 minute.

2. Add the tomatoes and their liquid, olives, capers, and anchovies and stir, pressing down on the anchovies to break them up. Cook until the anchovies have dissolved. Stir in the red pepper flakes, season with salt and pepper, and raise the heat to medium. Simmer, stirring occasionally, until the sauce thickens slightly, about 10 minutes. Taste and adjust seasoning if necessary before serving.

Creamy Gorgonzola Sauce with Candied Walnuts

YIELD: **3 CUPS**

ACTIVE TIME: **12 MINUTES**

TOTAL TIME: **25 MINUTES**

INGREDIENTS

1 TABLESPOON OLIVE OIL

1 TEASPOON STEAK SEASONING

1 TABLESPOON HONEY

½ TABLESPOON WATER

1 CUP WALNUTS

1 TABLESPOON SUGAR

SALT AND WHITE PEPPER, TO TASTE

⅛ TEASPOON CAYENNE PEPPER

2 CUPS HEAVY CREAM

1 CUP CHOPPED GORGONZOLA DOLCE CHEESE, CHOPPED

¾ CUP GRATED PARMESAN CHEESE

1 TEASPOON FRESHLY GRATED NUTMEG

DIRECTIONS

1. Line a baking sheet with parchment paper. Place the olive oil in a large skillet and warm over medium heat. When the oil starts to shimmer, stir in the steak seasoning, honey, and water. Add the walnuts and stir until they are evenly coated. Sprinkle the sugar, salt, and cayenne over the walnuts and sauté until they start to brown, about 3 minutes. Remove and transfer to the parchment paper–lined baking sheet, making sure the walnuts are in a single layer. Let them cool completely.

2. Place the cream and cheeses in a medium saucepan and bring to a simmer over medium heat, stirring occasionally. Cook until the sauce has reduced by one-third, about 8 minutes.

3. Stir in the nutmeg, season the sauce with salt and white pepper, and serve over pasta. Top with the candied walnuts.

NOTE: Gorgonzola dolce is aged less than regular gorgonzola, giving it a milder flavor.

Lamb Ragù

INGREDIENTS

2 TABLESPOONS OLIVE OIL

2 SMALL ONIONS, MINCED

2 CELERY STALKS, MINCED

SALT AND PEPPER, TO TASTE

2 LBS. GROUND LAMB

1 CUP DRY RED WINE

3 TABLESPOONS FINELY CHOPPED
FRESH THYME

2 TABLESPOONS FINELY CHOPPED
FRESH MARJORAM

1 SMALL DRIED CHILI PEPPER,
CHOPPED

2 (28 OZ.) CANS OF PEELED
WHOLE SAN MARZANO TOMATOES,
WITH THEIR LIQUID AND
CRUSHED BY HAND

DIRECTIONS

1. Place the olive oil in a Dutch oven and warm it over medium-high heat. When the oil starts to shimmer, add the onions, celery, and a couple of pinches of salt and stir to combine. When the mixture starts to sizzle, reduce the heat to low, cover the pan, and cook, stirring occasionally, until the vegetables are very tender and browned, about 30 minutes.

2. Add the ground lamb to the pot and cook, breaking it up with a fork, until it is browned. Raise the heat to medium-high, stir in the wine, and cook for 5 minutes. Add the thyme, marjoram, and chili pepper and cook for 2 minutes. Stir in the tomatoes and their liquid, season with salt and pepper, and bring the sauce to a boil. Reduce the heat to medium-low and simmer, stirring occasionally, until the sauce has noticeably thickened and separated, with the fat bubbling on the surface, about 2 hours. Taste and season if necessary before serving.

YIELD: **4 CUPS**

ACTIVE TIME: **45 MINUTES**

TOTAL TIME: **2 HOURS AND 30 MINUTES**

Rabbit Ragù

INGREDIENTS

¼ CUP OLIVE OIL

2½- TO 3½-LB. RABBIT, CUT INTO 8 BONE-IN PIECES

SALT AND PEPPER, TO TASTE

1 CUP ALL-PURPOSE FLOUR

1 YELLOW ONION, CHOPPED

2 CELERY STALKS, CHOPPED

2 CARROTS, PEELED AND CHOPPED

1 GARLIC CLOVE, MINCED

2 TABLESPOONS TOMATO PASTE

½ CUP DRY RED WINE

1 (28 OZ.) CAN OF CRUSHED TOMATOES, WITH THEIR LIQUID

1 CUP CHICKEN STOCK (SEE PAGE 109)

2 BAY LEAVES

2 SPRIGS OF FRESH ROSEMARY

4 SPRIGS OF FRESH THYME

DIRECTIONS

1. Place the olive oil in a Dutch oven and warm it over medium heat. Season the rabbit with salt and pepper, dredge the pieces in the flour, and shake to remove any excess. When the oil starts to shimmer, add the rabbit and cook until it is browned on both sides, about 4 minutes per side.

2. Use a slotted spoon to remove the rabbit and set it aside. Add the onion, celery, carrots, and garlic and sauté until the onion starts to brown, about 8 minutes. Stir in the tomato paste and cook for another 4 minutes.

3. Add the wine and let the mixture come to a rolling boil. Reduce the heat so that the sauce simmers and cook until the wine has reduced by half, about 10 minutes.

4. Stir in the tomatoes, stock, bay leaves, rosemary, and thyme and simmer for 2 minutes. Return the rabbit to the pot and simmer until it is extremely tender, about 1½ hours.

5. Use a slotted spoon to remove the rabbit and set it aside. Remove the bay leaves, rosemary, and thyme. When the rabbit is cool enough to handle, remove the meat from the bones and shred it. Discard the bones and return the meat to the sauce before serving over pasta.

Bolognese Sauce

INGREDIENTS

2 TABLESPOONS OLIVE OIL

½ LB. BACON

1½ LBS. GROUND BEEF

SALT AND PEPPER, TO TASTE

1 ONION, CHOPPED

1 CARROT, PEELED AND MINCED

3 CELERY STALKS, CHOPPED

2 GARLIC CLOVES, MINCED

1 TABLESPOON FINELY CHOPPED FRESH THYME

2 CUPS SHERRY

8 CUPS MARINARA SAUCE (SEE PAGE 67)

1 CUP WATER

1 CUP HEAVY CREAM

2 TABLESPOONS FINELY CHOPPED FRESH SAGE

1 CUP GRATED PARMESAN CHEESE

DIRECTIONS

1. Place the olive oil in a Dutch oven and warm over medium heat. When the oil starts to shimmer, add the bacon and cook until it is crispy, about 6 minutes. Add the ground beef, season it with salt and pepper, and cook, breaking up the meat with a fork as it browns, until it is cooked through, about 8 minutes. Remove the bacon and the ground beef from the pot and set them aside.

2. Add the onion, carrot, celery, and garlic to the Dutch oven, season with salt, and sauté until the carrot is tender, about 8 minutes. Return the bacon and ground beef to the pot, add the thyme and sherry, and cook until the sherry has nearly evaporated. Stir in the Marinara Sauce and water, reduce the heat to low, and cook for approximately 45 minutes, stirring often, until the sauce has thickened noticeably.

3. Stir the cream and sage into the sauce and cook for an additional 15 minutes.

4. Add the Parmesan and stir until melted. Taste and adjust the seasoning if necessary before serving.

YIELD: **2 CUPS**

ACTIVE TIME: **15 MINUTES**

TOTAL TIME: **45 MINUTES**

Creamy Leek Sauce

INGREDIENTS

4 LEEKS

4 TABLESPOONS UNSALTED BUTTER

SALT, TO TASTE

1¼ CUPS HEAVY CREAM

½ CUP WHOLE MILK

½ TEASPOON WHITE PEPPER

DIRECTIONS

1. Trim away the ends and dark green leaves of the leeks, keeping only the white and light green parts. With a sharp knife, cut each leek in half lengthwise and remove the two outer layers. Cut the halves into long, thin slivers, place them in a large bowl of water, and swish them around to remove any dirt. Drain well and pat the leeks dry.

2. Place the butter in a large skillet and melt it over medium heat. Add the leeks and a couple pinches of salt and sauté the leeks until translucent, about 3 minutes. Reduce the heat to low, cover the pan, and cook, stirring occasionally, until the leeks are very tender, about 20 minutes.

3. Raise the heat to medium-high, stir in the cream, milk, and white pepper and bring the sauce to a boil. Reduce the heat to low and simmer, uncovered, until the sauce has reduced slightly, about 5 minutes. Taste and adjust the seasoning if necessary before serving.

Gingery Red Pepper Sauce

YIELD: **2 CUPS**

ACTIVE TIME: **10 MINUTES**

TOTAL TIME: **30 MINUTES**

INGREDIENTS

2 RED BELL PEPPERS, STEMMED, SEEDS AND RIBS REMOVED, AND CHOPPED

1-INCH PIECE OF FRESH GINGER, PEELED AND CHOPPED

4 GARLIC CLOVES

3 TABLESPOONS SUGAR

2 TABLESPOONS TOMATO PASTE

1 TABLESPOON OLIVE OIL

1 TABLESPOON APPLE CIDER VINEGAR

1 TABLESPOON SOY SAUCE

DIRECTIONS

1. Place all of the ingredients in a food processor and blitz until pureed.

2. Transfer the mixture to a small saucepan and cook over medium heat, stirring occasionally, until it has reduced to the consistency of a thick tomato sauce, about 20 minutes. Taste and adjust the seasoning if necessary before seasoning.

Roasted Tomato & Garlic Sauce

YIELD: **6 CUPS**

ACTIVE TIME: **15 MINUTES**

TOTAL TIME: **2 HOURS**

INGREDIENTS

3 LBS. TOMATOES, HALVED

¼ CUP OLIVE OIL

5 LARGE GARLIC CLOVES, UNPEELED

SALT AND PEPPER, TO TASTE

1 HANDFUL OF FRESH BASIL LEAVES

DIRECTIONS

1. Preheat the oven to 350°F. Place the tomatoes on a parchment-lined baking sheet and drizzle the olive oil over them. Stir to ensure the tomatoes are coated evenly, place them in the oven, and lower the oven's temperature to 325°F. Roast the tomatoes for 1 hour.

2. Remove the baking sheet from the oven, place the garlic on the baking sheet, return it to the oven, and roast for another 30 minutes.

3. Remove the sheet from the oven and let them cool. Once cool enough to handle, remove the skins from the garlic cloves. Season the tomatoes and garlic with salt and pepper.

4. Place the tomatoes, garlic, and basil leaves in a food processor and blitz until pureed. Place the puree in a medium saucepan and bring to a simmer over medium heat, stirring occasionally. Taste and adjust the seasoning if necessary before serving with pasta.

Tomato & Eggplant Sauce alla Norma

YIELD: **6 CUPS**

ACTIVE TIME: **40 MINUTES**

TOTAL TIME: **1 HOUR AND 30 MINUTES**

INGREDIENTS

2 EGGPLANTS, CHOPPED

2 TABLESPOONS SALT, PLUS MORE TO TASTE

3 TABLESPOONS OLIVE OIL

5 CUPS MARINARA SAUCE (SEE PAGE 67)

1 CUP RICOTTA CHEESE

BLACK PEPPER, TO TASTE

DIRECTIONS

1. Place the eggplants in a colander and sprinkle the salt over them. Let rest for 30 minutes, rinse the eggplants, and pat them dry with paper towels.

2. Preheat the oven to 400°F. Place the eggplants in a large mixing bowl, drizzle the olive oil over them, and stir to make sure the pieces are evenly coated. Place the eggplants on a parchment-lined baking sheet, place it in the oven, and roast, stirring occasionally, until the eggplants are tender and golden brown, about 25 minutes. Remove from the oven and let the eggplants cool.

3. Place the eggplants, sauce, ricotta cheese, and basil in a large saucepan, stir to combine, and bring to a simmer over medium heat. Taste and adjust the seasoning if necessary before serving with pasta.

Sofia's Spiced Pork Sauce

INGREDIENTS

6 TABLESPOONS UNSALTED BUTTER

1 YELLOW ONION, GRATED

2 CELERY STALKS, GRATED

SALT, TO TASTE

1½ LBS. GROUND PORK

1 CUP MILK

½ TEASPOON GROUND CLOVES

1 CUP CHICKEN STOCK (SEE PAGE 109)

2 TABLESPOONS TOMATO PASTE

2 BAY LEAVES

6 FRESH SAGE LEAVES

DIRECTIONS

1. Place half of the butter in a large saucepan and melt it over medium-high heat. Add the onion, celery, and a few pinches of salt and sauté until the onion is translucent, about 3 minutes. Reduce the heat to low, cover the pan, and cook, stirring occasionally, until the vegetables are very tender, about 30 minutes.

2. Add the ground pork to the pan and raise the heat to medium-high. Season the pork with salt and cook, using a fork to break it up as it browns. When the pork is browned all over, stir in the milk and cook until the milk has completely evaporated, about 10 minutes.

3. Stir in the cloves, cook for 2 minutes, and then add the stock, tomato paste, and bay leaves. Bring the sauce to a boil, reduce the heat to low, and let the sauce simmer, stirring occasionally, until the flavor has developed to your liking, about 45 minutes.

4. Place the remaining butter in a small skillet and melt it over medium-low heat. Add the sage leaves and cook until the leaves are slightly crispy. Remove the sage leaves and discard them. Stir the seasoned butter into the sauce, taste, and adjust the seasoning if necessary.

Shrimp & Pistou Sauce

INGREDIENTS

1½ LBS. SHRIMP, PEELED AND
DEVEINED

4 GARLIC CLOVES

5 TABLESPOONS TOMATO PASTE

SALT AND PEPPER, TO TASTE

½ CUP GRATED PARMESAN CHEESE

2 HANDFULS OF FRESH BASIL
LEAVES, TORN

6 TABLESPOONS OLIVE OIL

3 CUPS MARINARA SAUCE (SEE
PAGE 67)

½ CUP WATER

DIRECTIONS

1. Place the shrimp on a paper towel–lined plate and let them come to room temperature. Place the garlic, tomato paste, and a generous pinch of salt in a food processor and pulse until thoroughly combined. Add the Parmesan and pulse to incorporate. Add the basil and pulse once. Transfer the mixture to a small bowl and whisk in ¼ cup of the olive oil. Set the pistou aside.

2. Place the remaining olive oil in a large, deep skillet and warm it over medium heat. Pat the shrimp dry with paper towels. When the oil starts to shimmer, add the shrimp to the pan, working in batches to ensure there is plenty of room between them. Cook for 2 minutes on each side, transfer the cooked shrimp to a plate, and tent it with aluminum foil.

3. Place the sauce and water in the skillet and bring to a simmer over medium-high heat. Stir in the pistou, taste, and season with salt and pepper. Serve the sauce over pasta and top with the cooked shrimp.

YIELD: **4 CUPS**

ACTIVE TIME: **5 MINUTES**

TOTAL TIME: **15 MINUTES**

Béchamel Sauce

INGREDIENTS

1 STICK OF UNSALTED BUTTER

½ CUP ALL-PURPOSE FLOUR

4 CUPS WHOLE MILK

½ TEASPOON FRESHLY GRATED NUTMEG

SALT AND WHITE PEPPER, TO TASTE

DIRECTIONS

1. Place the butter in a medium saucepan and melt it over medium heat, making sure it does not brown. Add the flour and stir until the mixture becomes velvety. Cook, stirring constantly, for 5 minutes, until the mixture stops foaming and turns golden brown.

2. Add ½ cup of the milk and stir vigorously until you've loosened the mixture. Incorporate the rest of the milk and cook, stirring constantly, until the mixture starts to thicken.

3. Stir in the nutmeg and season with salt and pepper. Taste and adjust the seasoning if necessary before serving.

TIP: Béchamel is perfect to inject some life into leftover pasta that utilizes a tomato-based sauce.

CHAPTER 3

SOUPS

Pasta and soup are two go-to dishes when we're in need of comfort. So it should come as no surprise that combining them provides unprecedented consolation. This chapter is brimming with simple, delicious standards that place pasta front and center to provide you with a host of solutions, whether you're seeking shelter from harsh weather or trying to cobble something satisfying together from the odds and ends in your pantry.

YIELD: **6 SERVINGS**

ACTIVE TIME: **30 MINUTES**

TOTAL TIME: **1 HOUR**

Harira

INGREDIENTS

3 TABLESPOONS UNSALTED BUTTER

1 LB. BONELESS, SKINLESS CHICKEN THIGHS

SALT AND PEPPER, TO TASTE

1 LARGE ONION, CHOPPED FINE

5 GARLIC CLOVES, MINCED

1-INCH PIECE OF FRESH GINGER, PEELED AND GRATED

2 TEASPOONS TURMERIC

1 TEASPOON CUMIN

½ TEASPOON CINNAMON

⅛ TEASPOON CAYENNE PEPPER

¾ CUP FINELY CHOPPED FRESH CILANTRO

½ CUP FINELY CHOPPED FRESH PARSLEY

4 CUPS CHICKEN STOCK (SEE PAGE 109)

4 CUPS WATER

1 (14 OZ.) CAN OF CHICKPEAS, DRAINED AND RINSED

1 CUP BROWN LENTILS, PICKED OVER AND RINSED

1 (28 OZ.) CAN OF CRUSHED TOMATOES, DRAINED

½ CUP SPAGHETTI, BROKEN INTO 2-INCH PIECES

2 TABLESPOONS FRESH LEMON JUICE, PLUS MORE TO TASTE

DIRECTIONS

1. Place the butter in a Dutch oven and melt it over medium-high heat. Season the chicken thighs with salt and pepper, place them in the pot, and cook until browned on both sides, about 8 minutes. Remove the chicken from the pot and set it on a plate.

2. Add the onion and sauté until it starts to brown, about 8 minutes. Add the garlic and ginger and cook until fragrant, about 1 minute. Stir in the turmeric, cumin, cinnamon, and cayenne pepper and cook for 1 minute. Add ½ cup of the cilantro and ¼ cup of the parsley and cook for 1 minute.

3. Stir in the stock, water, chickpeas, and lentils and bring the soup to a simmer. Return the chicken to the pot, reduce the heat to medium-low, partially cover the Dutch oven, and gently simmer, stirring occasionally, until the lentils are just tender, about 20 minutes.

4. Add the tomatoes and spaghetti and simmer, stirring occasionally, until the pasta is tender, about 10 minutes. Stir in the lemon juice and the remaining cilantro and parsley. Taste, adjust seasoning if necessary, and serve.

YIELD: **4 SERVINGS**

ACTIVE TIME: **1 HOUR**

TOTAL TIME: **1 HOUR AND 15 MINUTES**

Pantrucas in Broth

INGREDIENTS

2 CUPS ALL-PURPOSE FLOUR, PLUS
MORE AS NEEDED

1 TEASPOON SALT, PLUS MORE
TO TASTE

⅔ CUP LUKEWARM WATER (90°F),
PLUS MORE AS NEEDED

2 LARGE EGGS

1 TABLESPOON VEGETABLE OIL

2 LARGE EGG YOLKS

8 CUPS CHICKEN STOCK
(SEE SIDEBAR)

BLACK PEPPER, TO TASTE

1 HANDFUL OF FRESH CILANTRO,
CHOPPED, FOR GARNISH

DIRECTIONS

1. Place the flour and salt in a large bowl and stir to combine. Add the water, eggs, and vegetable oil and work the mixture with a wooden spoon until it starts to stick together. Work the dough with your hands and knead it until it becomes uniform, soft, and smooth, about 10 minutes. If the dough is too dry, incorporate more water, 1 teaspoon at a time.

2. Place the dough on a flour-dusted work surface and roll it into a thick log. Cut the log into 10 pieces, leave one piece out, and cover the rest with plastic wrap. Shape the piece of dough into a ball and press down to flatten it into a patty. Start rolling the dough with a flour-dusted rolling pin, turning it 45 degrees following each pass to ensure that it remains round. Once the dough is ⅛ inch thick, cut it into 1½-inch-wide strips. Cut the strips into 1½-inch squares. Arrange the squares in a single layer on a flour-dusted, parchment-lined baking sheet. Once you run out of room on the sheet, cover the squares with another sheet of parchment paper, lightly dust it with flour, and repeat the process until all of the pieces of dough have been turned into squares.

3. Place the egg yolks and 2 tablespoons of water in a small bowl and whisk to combine. Place the stock in a large pot and bring it to a gentle boil. Add the pasta and cook until tender yet chewy, about 10 minutes. Remove the pot from heat and stir in the egg mixture.

4. Ladle the soup into warmed bowls and top each portion with some of the cilantro.

CHICKEN STOCK

Place 3 lbs. rinsed chicken bones in a large stockpot, cover them with water, and bring to a boil. Add 1 chopped onion, 2 chopped carrots, 3 chopped celery stalks, 3 unpeeled, smashed garlic cloves, 3 sprigs of fresh thyme, 1 teaspoon black peppercorns, and 1 bay leaf, season the stock with salt, and reduce the heat so that the stock simmers. Cook for 2 hours, skimming to remove any impurities that float to the surface. Strain the stock through a fine sieve, let the stock cool slightly, and place it in the refrigerator, uncovered, to chill. Remove the fat layer and cover. The stock will keep in the refrigerator for 3 to 5 days, and in the freezer for up to 3 months.

Pasta e Fagioli

INGREDIENTS

2 TABLESPOONS OLIVE OIL

1 LB. PORK SPARERIBS, CUT INTO 4 PIECES

SALT AND PEPPER, TO TASTE

1 ONION, MINCED

1 CELERY STALK, MINCED

3 CARROTS, PEELED AND CHOPPED

3 GARLIC CLOVES, SLICED THIN

3 ANCHOVY FILLETS IN OLIVE OIL

1 (28 OZ.) CAN OF PEELED WHOLE SAN MARZANO TOMATOES, WITH THEIR LIQUID AND CRUSHED BY HAND

1 PARMESAN CHEESE RIND (OPTIONAL)

3 (14 OZ.) CANS OF CANNELLINI BEANS, DRAINED AND RINSED

6½ CUPS CHICKEN STOCK (SEE PAGE 109)

½ LB. PASTA

¼ CUP FINELY CHOPPED FRESH PARSLEY

1 CUP GRATED PARMESAN CHEESE

DIRECTIONS

1. Place the olive oil in a Dutch oven and warm it over medium-high heat. Season the spareribs with salt and pepper. When the oil starts to shimmer, place the spareribs in the pot and sauté, turning them as they cook, until browned all over, about 8 minutes. Transfer the spareribs to a plate and let them cool. When cool enough to handle, chop the spareribs into bite-sized pieces.

2. Reduce the heat to medium, add the onion, celery, carrots, and a couple pinches of salt and sauté until the onion turns translucent, about 3 minutes. Reduce the heat to low, cover the pot, and cook, stirring occasionally, until the vegetables are very soft, about 20 minutes.

3. Stir in the garlic and anchovies and sauté until the anchovies dissolve, about 1 minute. Add the tomatoes and their juices and scrape up any browned bits from the bottom of the pot. Raise the heat to medium-high, add the Parmesan rind (if using), beans, and stock and bring the soup to a boil. Reduce the heat to low and simmer, stirring occasionally, until the flavors have developed to your liking, about 45 minutes.

4. Remove the Parmesan rind and discard it. Return the spareribs to the pot and stir in the pasta. Cook until it is tender but still chewy, about 10 minutes. Remove the pot from heat, season with salt and pepper, and top with the parsley and Parmesan.

Chicken Soup with Meatballs, Farfalle, and Spinach

YIELD: **8 SERVINGS**

ACTIVE TIME: **35 MINUTES**

TOTAL TIME: **1 HOUR**

INGREDIENTS

FOR THE MEATBALLS

1 CUP FRESH BREAD CRUMBS

1 LB. GROUND CHICKEN

1 CUP GRATED PARMESAN CHEESE

3 TABLESPOONS TOMATO PASTE

1 HANDFUL OF FRESH PARSLEY, CHOPPED

3 LARGE EGGS

SALT AND PEPPER, TO TASTE

2 TABLESPOONS OLIVE OIL

FOR THE SOUP

2 TABLESPOONS OLIVE OIL

2 LEEKS, TRIMMED, RINSED WELL, AND CHOPPED

SALT AND PEPPER, TO TASTE

5 GARLIC CLOVES, SLICED THIN

8 CUPS CHICKEN STOCK (SEE PAGE 109)

Continued…

DIRECTIONS

1. To begin preparations for the meatballs, place the bread crumbs, chicken, Parmesan, tomato paste, parsley, and eggs in a mixing bowl, season the mixture with salt and pepper, and work the mixture with your hands until thoroughly combined. Working with wet hands, form the mixture into ½-inch balls.

2. Place the olive oil in a large skillet and warm it over medium heat. When the oil starts to shimmer, add the meatballs in batches and cook, turning them occasionally, until browned all over, about 8 minutes per batch. Transfer the cooked meatballs to a paper towel–lined plate to drain.

3. To begin preparations for the soup, place the olive oil in a Dutch oven and warm it over medium heat. When the oil starts to shimmer, add the leeks, season them with salt and pepper, and sauté until translucent, about 3 minutes. Reduce the heat to low, cover the pot, and cook, stirring occasionally, until the leeks are very soft, about 15 minutes.

4. Add the garlic, cook for 1 minute, and then stir in the stock, carrots, and meatballs. Raise the heat and bring the soup to a gentle boil. Reduce the heat to medium-low and simmer the soup until the meatballs are cooked through and the carrots are tender, about 15 minutes.

Continued…

5 CARROTS, PEELED AND SLICED

½ LB. FARFALLE (SEE PAGE 31)

2 HANDFULS OF BABY SPINACH LEAVES

¼ CUP GRATED PARMESAN CHEESE, PLUS MORE FOR GARNISH

5. Add the Farfalle and cook until tender, about 2 minutes. Remove the Dutch oven from heat and stir in the spinach and Parmesan. Cover the pot and let it rest until the spinach has wilted, about 5 minutes. Ladle the soup into warmed bowls and garnish each portion with additional Parmesan.

YIELD: **4 SERVINGS**

ACTIVE TIME: **45 MINUTES**

TOTAL TIME: **1 HOUR AND 15 MINUTES**

Meatball & Orzo Soup

INGREDIENTS

FOR THE MEATBALLS

2 SLICES OF WHITE BREAD, CRUSTS REMOVED, TORN INTO SMALL PIECES

6 TABLESPOONS MILK

¾ LB. GROUND CHICKEN

½ ONION, CHOPPED

3 TABLESPOONS FINELY CHOPPED FRESH PARSLEY

1 TABLESPOON ORANGE ZEST

2 GARLIC CLOVES, MINCED

1 EGG, BEATEN

SALT AND PEPPER, TO TASTE

2 TABLESPOONS OLIVE OIL

Continued...

DIRECTIONS

1. To begin preparations for the meatballs, place the bread and milk in a bowl and let the mixture rest for 10 minutes.

2. Add the chicken, onion, parsley, orange zest, garlic, and egg and work the mixture with your hands until thoroughly combined. Season with salt and pepper and form the mixture into 1-inch balls.

3. Place the oil in a large skillet and warm it over medium heat. When it starts to shimmer, add the meatballs and cook, turning them occasionally, until they are browned all over, about 8 minutes. Transfer to a paper towel–lined plate to drain.

4. To begin preparations for the soup, place the cannellini beans and 1 cup of the stock in a food processor, blitz until pureed, and set the mixture aside. Place the olive oil in a saucepan and warm it over medium heat. When the oil starts to shimmer, add the onion, garlic, chili, celery, and carrot and sauté until the vegetables start to soften, about 5 minutes.

5. Stir in the tomato paste, the cannellini puree, and the remaining stock and bring the soup to a boil. Reduce the heat so that the soup simmers and cook for 10 minutes.

6. Add the orzo and cook until it is tender, about 8 minutes. Add the meatballs, cook until cooked through, and then season the soup with salt and pepper. Ladle the soup into warmed bowls and garnish with the Pecorino and basil.

FOR THE SOUP

1 (14 OZ.) CAN OF CANNELLINI BEANS, DRAINED AND RINSED

4 CUPS CHICKEN STOCK (SEE PAGE 109)

2 TABLESPOONS OLIVE OIL

1 ONION, CHOPPED

1 GARLIC CLOVE, MINCED

1 BIRD'S EYE CHILI PEPPER, STEMMED, SEEDS AND RIBS REMOVED, AND CHOPPED

1 CELERY STALK, CHOPPED

1 CARROT, PEELED AND CHOPPED

1 TABLESPOON TOMATO PASTE

1½ CUPS ORZO

SALT AND PEPPER, TO TASTE

PECORINO ROMANO CHEESE, GRATED, FOR GARNISH

FRESH BASIL, FINELY CHOPPED, FOR GARNISH

YIELD: **4 SERVINGS**

ACTIVE TIME: **30 MINUTES**

TOTAL TIME: **1 HOUR AND 15 MINUTES**

Italian Wedding Soup

INGREDIENTS

FOR THE MEATBALLS

¾ LB. GROUND CHICKEN

⅓ CUP PANKO

1 GARLIC CLOVE, MINCED

2 TABLESPOONS FINELY CHOPPED FRESH PARSLEY

¼ CUP GRATED PARMESAN CHEESE

1 TABLESPOON MILK

1 EGG, BEATEN

⅛ TEASPOON FENNEL SEEDS

⅛ TEASPOON RED PEPPER FLAKES

½ TEASPOON PAPRIKA

SALT AND PEPPER, TO TASTE

Continued...

DIRECTIONS

1. Preheat the oven to 350°F. To prepare the meatballs, place all of the ingredients in a mixing bowl and work the mixture with your hands until combined. Working with wet hands, form the mixture into 1-inch balls and place them on a parchment-lined baking sheet. Place the meatballs in the oven and bake for 12 to 15 minutes, until browned and cooked through. Remove from the oven and set the meatballs aside.

2. To begin preparations for the soup, place the olive oil in a saucepan and warm it over medium heat. When the oil starts to shimmer, add the onion, carrots, and celery and sauté until they start to soften, about 5 minutes.

3. Stir in the stock and the wine and bring the soup to a boil. Reduce the heat so that the soup simmers, add the pasta, and cook until it is tender, about 8 minutes.

4. Add the cooked meatballs and simmer for 5 minutes. Stir in the dill and the spinach and cook until the spinach has wilted, about 2 minutes. Season the soup with salt and pepper, ladle it into warmed bowls, and garnish with the Parmesan.

FOR THE SOUP

2 TABLESPOONS OLIVE OIL

1 ONION, CHOPPED

2 CARROTS, PEELED AND MINCED

1 CELERY STALK, MINCED

6 CUPS CHICKEN STOCK (SEE PAGE 109)

¼ CUP WHITE WINE

½ CUP TUBETINI

2 TABLESPOONS FINELY CHOPPED FRESH DILL

6 OZ. BABY SPINACH

SALT AND PEPPER, TO TASTE

PARMESAN CHEESE, GRATED, FOR GARNISH

Tomato Soup with Chickpeas & Ditalini

YIELD: **4 SERVINGS**

ACTIVE TIME: **20 MINUTES**

TOTAL TIME: **45 MINUTES**

INGREDIENTS

2 TABLESPOONS OLIVE OIL

1 ONION, CHOPPED

2 GARLIC CLOVES, MINCED

2 (28 OZ.) CANS OF STEWED TOMATOES, PUREED

2 TABLESPOONS FINELY CHOPPED FRESH THYME

4 CUPS CHICKEN STOCK (SEE PAGE 109)

½ CUP DITALINI

1 (14 OZ.) CAN OF CHICKPEAS, DRAINED AND RINSED

¼ CUP FINELY CHOPPED FRESH PARSLEY

¼ CUP GRATED PARMESAN CHEESE, PLUS MORE FOR GARNISH

SALT AND PEPPER, TO TASTE

FRESH BASIL, FINELY CHOPPED, FOR GARNISH

DIRECTIONS

1. Place the olive oil in a large saucepan and warm over medium heat. When the oil starts to shimmer, add the onion and sauté until it starts to soften, about 5 minutes. Add the garlic, cook for 1 minute, and then stir in the pureed tomatoes, thyme, and stock.

2. Bring the soup to a boil, reduce the heat so that the soup simmers, and add the ditalini and chickpeas. Cook until the pasta is tender, about 8 minutes.

3. Stir in the parsley and Parmesan and cook until everything is warmed through, about 3 minutes. Season with salt and pepper, ladle into warmed bowls, and garnish with additional Parmesan and the basil.

Broccoli & Anchovy Soup

YIELD: **4 SERVINGS**

ACTIVE TIME: **20 MINUTES**

TOTAL TIME: **45 MINUTES**

INGREDIENTS

1 TABLESPOON OLIVE OIL

1 TABLESPOON UNSALTED BUTTER

1 ONION, CHOPPED

1 GARLIC CLOVE, MINCED

1½ CUPS CHOPPED PORTOBELLO MUSHROOMS

1 BIRD'S EYE CHILI PEPPER, STEMMED, SEEDS AND RIBS REMOVED, AND CHOPPED

2 ANCHOVY FILLETS IN OLIVE OIL, MINCED

2 TOMATOES, PEELED, SEEDED, AND CHOPPED

¼ CUP WHITE WINE

4 CUPS VEGETABLE STOCK (SEE PAGE 125)

2 CUPS BROCCOLI FLORETS

½ LB. ORECCHIETTE (SEE PAGE 32)

SALT AND PEPPER, TO TASTE

PARMESAN CHEESE, GRATED, FOR GARNISH

DIRECTIONS

1. Place the olive oil and butter in a saucepan and warm over low heat. When the butter has melted, add the onion, garlic, mushrooms, chili, and anchovies and sauté until the onion starts to soften, about 5 minutes.

2. Stir in the tomatoes and the white wine and simmer, stirring occasionally, for 10 minutes.

3. Add the stock, raise the heat to medium-high, and bring the soup to a boil. Reduce the heat so that the soup simmers. Add the broccoli florets and pasta cook until they are tender, about 10 minutes.

4. Season with salt and pepper, ladle the soup into warmed bowls, and garnish with Parmesan cheese.

YIELD: **4 SERVINGS**

ACTIVE TIME: **15 MINUTES**

TOTAL TIME: **30 MINUTES**

Avgolemono

INGREDIENTS

6 CUPS CHICKEN STOCK (SEE PAGE 109)

½ CUP ORZO

3 EGGS

1 TABLESPOON FRESH LEMON JUICE

1 TABLESPOON COLD WATER

1½ CUPS CHOPPED LEFTOVER CHICKEN

SALT AND PEPPER, TO TASTE

LEMON SLICES, FOR GARNISH

FRESH PARSLEY, FINELY CHOPPED, FOR GARNISH

DIRECTIONS

1. Place the stock in a large saucepan and bring it to a boil. Reduce heat so that the stock simmers, add the orzo, and cook until it is tender, about 5 minutes.

2. Strain the stock and orzo over a large bowl. Set the orzo aside. Return the stock to the pan and bring it to a simmer.

3. Place the eggs in a mixing bowl and beat until they are scrambled and frothy. Stir in the lemon juice and cold water. While stirring constantly, incorporate approximately ½ cup of the stock into the mixture. Stir another cup of stock into the egg mixture and then stir the tempered eggs into the saucepan. Be careful not to let the stock come to boil once you add the tempered eggs.

4. Add the chicken and return the orzo to the soup. Cook, while stirring, until everything is warmed through, about 5 minutes. Season with salt and pepper, ladle into warmed bowls, and garnish with the slices of lemon and the parsley.

Cream of Mushroom

INGREDIENTS

4 TABLESPOONS UNSALTED BUTTER

1 ONION, CHOPPED

2 GARLIC CLOVES, CHOPPED

⅓ CUP MADEIRA WINE

¾ LB. WILD MUSHROOMS

4 CUPS VEGETABLE STOCK
(SEE SIDEBAR)

1½ CUPS FUSILLI PASTA

1 CUP HEAVY CREAM

SALT AND PEPPER, TO TASTE

FRESH PARSLEY, FINELY CHOPPED,
FOR GARNISH

DIRECTIONS

1. Place the butter in a large saucepan and melt it over medium heat. Add the onion and garlic and sauté until the onion starts to soften, about 5 minutes.

2. Stir in the Madeira and cook until it has evaporated, about 5 minutes. Add the mushrooms and cook until they have released all of their liquid and start to brown, about 10 minutes.

3. Add the stock and bring the soup to a boil. Reduce the heat so that it simmers and cook for 10 minutes.

4. Transfer the soup to a blender, puree until smooth and creamy, and then strain through a fine sieve.

5. Return the soup to a clean saucepan and bring it to a simmer. Add the fusilli and cook until it is tender, about 8 minutes.

6. Add the heavy cream and simmer for 2 minutes while stirring constantly. Season with salt and pepper, ladle the soup into warmed bowls, and garnish with parsley.

NOTE: Fusilli is recommended because it has the ideal texture for this soup. But feel free to substitute your favorite pasta, or whatever's in the cupboard.

VEGETABLE STOCK

Place 2 tablespoons olive oil, 2 trimmed and well rinsed leeks, 2 peeled and sliced carrots, 2 celery stalks, 2 sliced onions, and 3 unpeeled, smashed garlic cloves in a large stockpot and cook over low heat until the liquid the vegetables release has evaporated. Add 2 sprigs of fresh parsley and thyme, 1 bay leaf, 8 cups water, ½ teaspoon black peppercorns, and salt to taste. Raise the heat to high and bring the stock to a boil. Reduce heat so that the stock simmers and cook for 2 hours, skimming to remove any impurities that float to the surface. Strain the stock through a fine sieve, let the stock cool slightly, and place it in the refrigerator, uncovered, to chill. Remove the fat layer and cover. The stock will keep in the refrigerator for 3 to 5 days, and in the freezer for up to 3 months.

Beet Soup with Mushroom Ravioli

YIELD: **4 SERVINGS**

ACTIVE TIME: **1 HOUR**

TOTAL TIME: **1 HOUR AND 45 MINUTES**

INGREDIENTS

FOR THE RAVIOLI

1 TABLESPOON UNSALTED BUTTER

2 CUPS CHOPPED PORTOBELLO MUSHROOMS

1 SHALLOT, MINCED

1 GARLIC CLOVE, MINCED

LEAVES FROM 1 SPRIG OF FRESH THYME, CHOPPED

2 TABLESPOONS MASCARPONE CHEESE

SALT AND PEPPER, TO TASTE

RAVIOLI (SEE PAGE 27)

1 EGG, BEATEN

1 TABLESPOON WATER

FOR THE SOUP

1 TABLESPOON OLIVE OIL

1 ONION, CHOPPED

2 GARLIC CLOVES, MINCED

1 TEASPOON FENNEL SEEDS

1 LARGE BEET, PEELED AND MINCED

6 CUPS VEGETABLE STOCK (SEE PAGE 125)

¼ CUP ORANGE JUICE

SALT AND PEPPER, TO TASTE

DIRECTIONS

1. To begin preparations for the ravioli, place the butter in a medium saucepan and melt over medium heat. Add the mushrooms and cook until they start to release their liquid, about 5 minutes. Add the shallot, garlic, and thyme and cook until the shallot starts to soften, about 5 minutes. Remove the pan from heat and strain the mixture to remove any excess liquid. Let the mixture cool. Once it is cool, place in a small bowl and add the mascarpone. Stir to combine, season with salt and pepper, and set the filling aside.

2. Place a teaspoon of the filling into the depressions of the piece of dough laid over the ravioli tray. Combine the beaten egg and water in a small bowl. Dip a pastry brush or a finger into it the wash and lightly coat the edge of each ravioli.

3. Gently lay the other rectangle over the piece in the ravioli tray. Use a rolling pin to gently cut out the ravioli. Remove the cut ravioli and place them on a flour-dusted baking sheet.

4. To begin preparations for the soup, place the oil in a large saucepan and warm it over medium heat. When the oil starts to shimmer, add the onion, garlic, and fennel seeds and sauté until the onion starts to soften, about 5 minutes. Add the beet and cook for 5 minutes. Add the stock and orange juice, bring to a boil, then reduce heat so that the soup simmers. Cook until the beet is tender, about 15 minutes. Transfer the soup to a food processor and blitz until it is pureed.

Continued...

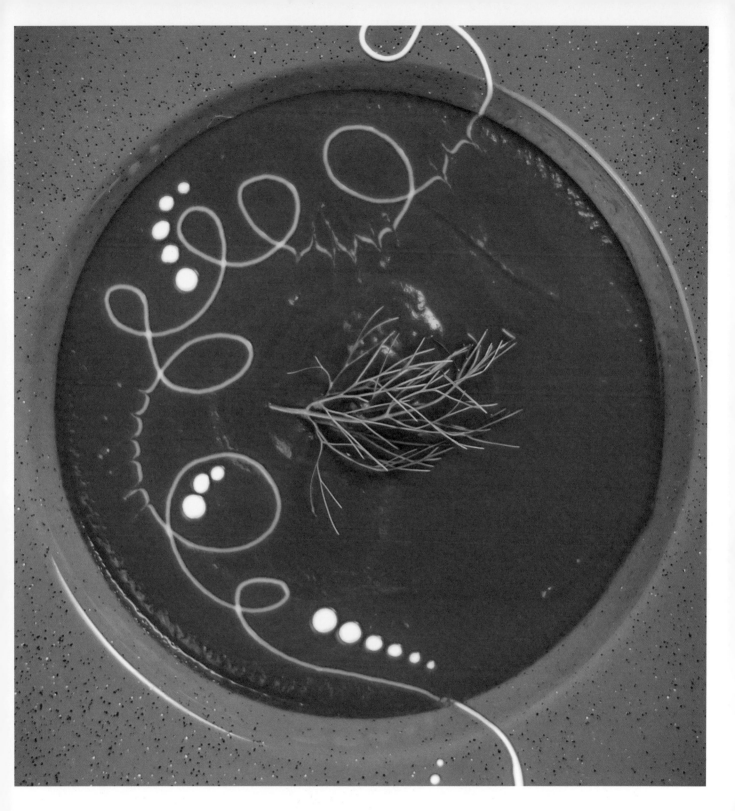

5. Place the soup in a clean saucepan, season it with salt and pepper, and return to a boil. Once boiling, drop the ravioli into the pan and cook for 3 minutes. Ladle the soup into shallow bowls.

TIP: Once you get some practice with making ravioli, try making some into heart shapes to serve a loved one—they'll look great against the vibrant color of the soup.

Chicken Liver & Farfalle Soup

YIELD: **4 SERVINGS**

ACTIVE TIME: **25 MINUTES**

TOTAL TIME: **1 HOUR**

INGREDIENTS

1 TABLESPOON OLIVE OIL

1 TABLESPOON UNSALTED BUTTER

½ CUP CHOPPED CHICKEN LIVERS

4 GARLIC CLOVES, MINCED

2 TABLESPOONS WHITE WINE

2 TABLESPOONS FINELY CHOPPED FRESH PARSLEY

2 TABLESPOONS FINELY CHOPPED FRESH MARJORAM

2 TABLESPOONS FINELY CHOPPED FRESH SAGE

1 TABLESPOON FINELY CHOPPED FRESH THYME

6 FRESH BASIL LEAVES, FINELY CHOPPED

6 CUPS CHICKEN STOCK (SEE PAGE 109)

2 CUPS PEAS

1 CUP FARFALLE (SEE PAGE 31 FOR HOMEMADE)

3 SCALLION WHITES, SLICED

SALT AND PEPPER, TO TASTE

DIRECTIONS

1. Place the oil and butter in a medium saucepan and warm over medium-high heat. When the butter has melted, add the chicken livers and garlic and sauté until the chicken livers are browned all over, about 5 minutes. Add the wine and cook until it evaporates. Stir in the herbs and cook for 2 minutes. Remove pan from heat and set aside.

2. Place the stock in a large saucepan and bring it to a boil. Reduce the heat so that the stock simmers, add the peas, and cook for 5 minutes.

3. Return the broth to a boil and add the Farfalle. Reduce the heat so that the broth simmers and cook until the pasta is al dente.

4. Add the chicken liver mixture and scallions and simmer for 3 minutes. Season the soup with salt and pepper and ladle it into warmed bowls.

Chicken Parm Soup

INGREDIENTS

2 TABLESPOONS OLIVE OIL

2 CHICKEN BREASTS, CUT
INTO ½-INCH PIECES

1 ONION, CHOPPED

2 GARLIC CLOVES, MINCED

1 TEASPOON RED PEPPER FLAKES

¼ CUP TOMATO PASTE

1 (14 OZ.) CAN OF DICED
TOMATOES, WITH THEIR LIQUID

6 CUPS CHICKEN STOCK (SEE
PAGE 109)

½ LB. PENNE

2 CUPS SHREDDED MOZZARELLA
CHEESE

1 CUP GRATED PARMESAN CHEESE,
PLUS MORE FOR GARNISH

SALT AND PEPPER, TO TASTE

FRESH BASIL, CHOPPED,
FOR GARNISH

DIRECTIONS

1. Place the olive oil in a medium saucepan and warm it over medium-high heat. When the oil starts to shimmer, add the chicken and sauté until it is browned all over, about 6 minutes.

2. Add the onion and garlic and sauté until the onion starts to soften, about 5 minutes. Stir in the red pepper flakes, tomato paste, tomatoes, and stock and bring the soup to a boil. Reduce heat so that the soup simmers and cook for 10 minutes.

3. Add the penne and cook until it is tender, about 10 minutes. Stir in the mozzarella and Parmesan and cook until they have melted. Season the soup with salt and pepper, ladle it into bowls, and garnish each portion with the basil and additional Parmesan.

CHAPTER 4

CLASSIC

DISHES

---

*Thanks to dishes like Spaghetti alla Carbonara (see page 159)
and Penne alla Vodka (see page 164), Italian food means pasta for many
people. And while that sells the incredible range of Italy's cuisine short—a
look at Marcella Hazan's seminal* Essentials of Classic Italian Cooking *will
show you the cost of such myopia—the beloved preparations that have been
gathered in this chapter make it more than understandable.*

Tarhana with Green Beans & Tomatoes

YIELD: **4 SERVINGS**

ACTIVE TIME: **30 MINUTES**

TOTAL TIME: **1 HOUR**

INGREDIENTS

6 PLUM TOMATOES

3 TABLESPOONS OLIVE OIL

1 ONION, MINCED

¼ TEASPOON KOSHER SALT, PLUS MORE TO TASTE

1 GARLIC CLOVE, MINCED

1½ LBS. FRESH GREEN BEANS, TRIMMED

1½ CUPS CHICKEN STOCK (SEE PAGE 109), PLUS MORE AS NEEDED

⅔ CUP TARHANA (SEE PAGE 62)

¼ CUP FRESH BASIL LEAVES, SHREDDED

BLACK PEPPER, TO TASTE

DIRECTIONS

1. Bring a medium saucepan of water to a boil. Add the tomatoes and parboil for 1 minute. Use tongs to transfer them to a cutting board and let them cool. When cool enough to handle, peel the tomatoes and discard the skins. Cut the flesh into quarters, remove the seeds and discard them, and mince the flesh.

2. Place the olive oil in a large, deep skillet and warm it over medium heat. When it begins to shimmer, add the onion and a couple pinches of salt and sauté until the onion is translucent, about 3 minutes. Reduce the heat to low, cover, and cook until the onion is very soft, about 15 minutes. Add the garlic and sauté for 1 minute. Stir in the tomatoes and a couple pinches of salt and raise the heat to medium-high. Once the sauce begins to bubble, reduce the heat to low, cover the pan, and cook, stirring occasionally, until the tomatoes start to collapse, about 10 minutes.

3. Add the green beans, stock, the ¼ teaspoon of salt, and the Tarhana. Raise the heat to medium-high and bring the mixture to a gentle simmer. Reduce heat to medium-low and cook, stirring occasionally, until the green beans and Tarhana are tender, 15 to 20 minutes. Add more stock as necessary.

4. Season to taste, stir in the basil and black pepper, and serve.

Butternut Squash Ravioli

YIELD: **4 SERVINGS**

ACTIVE TIME: **30 MINUTES**

TOTAL TIME: **1 HOUR AND 30 MINUTES**

INGREDIENTS

1½ LBS. BUTTERNUT SQUASH, HALVED LENGTHWISE AND SEEDED

OLIVE OIL, AS NEEDED

¼ CUP FRESH BREAD CRUMBS

½ CUP GRATED PARMESAN CHEESE, PLUS MORE FOR GARNISH

¼ CUP CRUMBLED GORGONZOLA CHEESE

2 EGG YOLKS, BEATEN

1 TEASPOON FRESHLY GRATED NUTMEG

10 FRESH ROSEMARY LEAVES, FINELY CHOPPED

RAVIOLI (SEE PAGE 27)

SALT, TO TASTE

CREAMY LEEK SAUCE (SEE PAGE 91), FOR SERVING

DIRECTIONS

1. Preheat the oven to 375°F. Brush the flesh of the squash with olive oil and place them, cut side up, on parchment-lined baking sheets. Place the squash in the oven and roast until fork-tender, 40 to 45 minutes. Remove from the oven and let cool, then scoop the flesh into a bowl and mash until smooth. Add the bread crumbs, cheeses, egg yolks, nutmeg, and rosemary to the squash and stir until thoroughly combined.

2. Bring a large saucepan of water to a boil and make the ravioli as instructed, filling the depressions with the butternut squash mixture.

3. When the water is boiling, add salt and the ravioli, stir to make sure they do not stick to the bottom, and cook until tender but still chewy, about 2 minutes. Drain, divide them between the serving plates, drizzle the Creamy Leek Sauce over the top, and garnish with additional Parmesan.

YIELD: **6 SERVINGS**

ACTIVE TIME: **15 MINUTES**

TOTAL TIME: **30 MINUTES**

Sopa de Fideo

INGREDIENTS

4 PLUM TOMATOES

2 CHIPOTLE PEPPERS IN ADOBO, SEEDED TO TASTE AND MINCED

1 TABLESPOON ADOBO SAUCE

2 GARLIC CLOVES, CHOPPED

SALT AND PEPPER, TO TASTE

¼ CUP OLIVE OIL

½ LB. FIDEO NOODLES

1 LARGE YELLOW ONION, CHOPPED

2 CUPS CHICKEN STOCK (SEE PAGE 109)

FLESH OF 1 AVOCADO, CHOPPED

1 HANDFUL OF FRESH CILANTRO, FOR GARNISH

DIRECTIONS

1. Bring water to a boil in a large saucepan and prepare an ice water bath. Add the tomatoes, parboil for 1 minute, remove them with tongs, and place them in the ice water bath. When the tomatoes are completely cool, peel them and place them in a food processor. Add the chipotles, adobo sauce, and garlic, season the mixture with salt and pepper, and blitz until pureed.

2. Place the olive oil in a large, deep skillet and warm over medium heat. When the oil begins to shimmer, add the pasta and sauté it until it is a deep golden brown, 5 to 7 minutes. Transfer the pasta to a paper towel–lined plate to drain.

3. Add the onion to the pan, season it with salt, and sauté until it is translucent, about 3 minutes. Reduce the heat to medium-low and cook until the onion is lightly browned, about 20 minutes. Stir in the stock, raise the heat to medium-high, and bring the mixture to a boil. Stir in the pasta, reduce the heat to the lowest setting, and cover the pan. Cook until the pasta has absorbed all of the liquid. Remove the pan from heat and let it sit for 5 minutes. Garnish with the avocado and cilantro before serving.

Vegetarian Rotolo

INGREDIENTS

5 TABLESPOONS PEANUT OIL

10 SCALLIONS, TRIMMED AND SLICED THIN

SALT, TO TASTE

1 LB. CREMINI MUSHROOMS, STEMMED AND MINCED

1 LB. EXTRA-FIRM TOFU, DRAINED AND CUT INTO ½-INCH SLICES

4 CUPS SHREDDED CABBAGE

4 CARROTS, PEELED AND GRATED

3 TABLESPOONS SOY SAUCE

3 TABLESPOONS WATER

2 TABLESPOONS SUGAR

1 TEASPOON WHITE PEPPER

4 TEASPOONS TOASTED SESAME OIL, PLUS MORE AS NEEDED

4 TEASPOONS CORNSTARCH

ALL-YOLK PASTA DOUGH (SEE PAGE 22), ROLLED ¹⁄₁₆ INCH THICK AND CUT INTO 15-INCH SHEETS

2 HANDFULS OF FRESH CILANTRO, CHOPPED, PLUS MORE FOR GARNISH

2 CUPS GINGERY RED PEPPER SAUCE (SEE PAGE 92), WARMED

DIRECTIONS

1. Place the peanut oil in a large skillet and warm it over medium heat. When it begins to shimmer, add the scallions and a pinch of salt and sauté until the scallions are translucent, about 3 minutes. Raise the heat to medium-high, add the mushrooms, tofu, cabbage, and carrots and sauté until all of the vegetables start to soften, about 5 minutes.

2. Place the soy sauce, 2 tablespoons of the water, the sugar, pepper, and sesame oil in a small bowl. Place the cornstarch and the remaining water in another bowl, whisk it until smooth, and then whisk it into the soy mixture. Stir the mixture into the skillet and raise the heat to high. Cook until the liquid has evaporated and the vegetables are cooked through, about 2 minutes. Remove the pan from heat and let the mixture cool slightly. Transfer it to a food processor and pulse until it is a chunky puree. Season with salt and set it aside.

3. Bring a large pot of water to a boil. Once it's boiling, add salt and add a single sheet of pasta. Cook for 1 minute, retrieve the sheet using two large slotted spoons, transfer to a kitchen towel, and let it cool. Repeat until all of the pasta sheets have been cooked.

Continued...

4. Preheat the oven to 475°F. Generously oil a 15 x 10-inch baking pan with sesame oil. Working with one pasta sheet at a time, lay it on a work surface covered with parchment paper. Using a rubber spatula, spread some of the puree over the sheet and sprinkle some of the cilantro on top. Starting at one short end, roll the sheet up tightly. Once you are done rolling, rest it on its seam to keep it from unrolling, or secure the roll with toothpicks. When all of the pasta sheets and filling have been used up, slice each roll into 1¼-inch-thick rounds. Place the rounds, facing upward, in the baking dish, making sure to leave space between. Place the pan in the oven and bake until lightly browned on top and heated through, 10 to 12 minutes.

5. To serve, place 2 to 3 tablespoons of the sauce on a warm plate, arrange three rotolo slices on top, and garnish with additional cilantro.

Rigatoni with Chickpeas

INGREDIENTS

3 TABLESPOONS OLIVE OIL, PLUS 1 TEASPOON

¼ CUP DICED PANCETTA

4 YELLOW ONIONS, SLICED THIN

SALT AND PEPPER, TO TASTE

1 TABLESPOON BALSAMIC VINEGAR

¾ LB. RIGATONI

1 (14 OZ.) CAN OF CHICKPEAS, DRAINED AND RINSED

FRESH ROSEMARY, FINELY CHOPPED, FOR GARNISH

DIRECTIONS

1. Add the 3 tablespoons of olive oil to a large skillet and warm over medium heat. When the oil starts to shimmer, add the pancetta and sauté until it begins to brown, about 5 minutes. Transfer the pancetta to a bowl and set it aside. Reduce the heat to medium-low, add the onions, and cook, stirring frequently, until the onions are caramelized, about 40 minutes. Season with salt and pepper and stir in the balsamic vinegar. Remove the pan from heat and cover it.

2. Bring a large pot of water to a boil. Add salt, the pasta, and chickpeas and cook 2 minutes short of the directed cooking time for the pasta. Reserve ¼ cup of the pasta water and drain the pasta and chickpeas. Return the empty pot to the stove, turn the heat to high, add the remaining olive oil and the reserved pasta water. Add the pasta and chickpeas and toss to combine. Stir in the pancetta and the onions and cook until the water has been absorbed, about 2 minutes. Garnish with the rosemary before serving.

Spaghetti alla Serena

INGREDIENTS

⅔ CUP MADEIRA WINE

8½ TABLESPOONS UNSALTED BUTTER

1 LB. CREMINI MUSHROOMS, QUARTERED

SALT AND WHITE PEPPER, TO TASTE

2 TABLESPOONS OLIVE OIL

1 SMALL YELLOW ONION, GRATED

1 RED BELL PEPPER, STEMMED, SEEDS AND RIBS REMOVED, AND SLICED THIN

1 CUP WHOLE MILK

1½ CUPS GRATED GRUYÈRE CHEESE

2 CUPS COOKED CHICKEN BREAST, SHREDDED

1 HANDFUL OF FRESH PARSLEY LEAVES, CHOPPED, PLUS MORE FOR GARNISH

¾ LB. SPAGHETTI

PARMESAN CHEESE, GRATED, FOR GARNISH

DIRECTIONS

1. Place the wine in a small saucepan, bring it to a boil, and cook until reduced by half, about 5 minutes. Remove the pan from the stove and set the reduced wine aside.

2. Place 2 tablespoons of the butter in a large skillet and melt it over medium-high heat. Add half of the mushrooms and a pinch of salt, and sauté until the mushrooms have softened and started to brown, about 8 minutes. Transfer to a bowl and cover it with aluminum foil. Melt another 2 tablespoons of the butter in the pan, add the remaining mushrooms, season them with salt, and sauté until they have softened and started to brown. Transfer them to the bowl containing the other mushrooms.

3. Bring a large pot of water to a boil. Add the olive oil to the skillet, reduce the heat to medium, and warm for 1 minute. Add the onion and sauté until it is translucent, about 3 minutes. Add the bell pepper and sauté until it is soft, about 10 minutes. Raise the heat to medium-high and cook until the bell pepper starts to brown, about 4 minutes.

4. Stir in the mushrooms, reduced wine, and the milk, bring to a boil, and reduce the heat to low. Add the remaining butter and the Gruyère and stir until melted. Add the chicken and parsley, season with salt and pepper, and cook, stirring occasionally, until the chicken is warmed through.

5. Add salt and the pasta to the boiling water and cook 1 minute short of the directed time. Reserve ½ cup of pasta water, drain the pasta, and return the pot to the stove. Add the reserved pasta water, turn the heat to high, add the pasta, and cook until it has absorbed the water. Transfer the pasta to the skillet and toss to combine. Season to taste and garnish with additional parsley and Parmesan.

Spaghetti alla Gricia

INGREDIENTS

½ LB. GUANCIALE, DICED

½ TEASPOON BLACK PEPPER, PLUS
MORE TO TASTE

SALT, TO TASTE

¾ LB. SPAGHETTI

1 TEASPOON OLIVE OIL

⅓ CUP GRATED PECORINO
ROMANO CHEESE, PLUS MORE
FOR GARNISH

DIRECTIONS

1. Place the guanciale in a large, deep skillet and cook over medium heat, stirring occasionally, until the fat renders and the edges start to brown, about 20 minutes. Stir in the pepper and remove the skillet from heat.

2. Bring a large pot of water to a boil. Add salt and the pasta and cook 1 minute less than the directed time. Reserve ¾ cup of pasta water, drain the pasta, and return the pot to the stove. Add reserved pasta water and the olive oil, raise the heat to high, add the pasta, and toss to combine.

3. Stir in the guanciale, its rendered fat, and the Pecorino and cook, tossing constantly, for 2 minutes. Season with salt and pepper and garnish with additional Pecorino.

Bucatini all'Amatriciana

INGREDIENTS

1 TABLESPOON OLIVE OIL, PLUS MORE AS NEEDED

4 OZ. GUANCIALE OR PANCETTA, DICED

2 DRIED RED CHILI PEPPERS, SEEDED TO TASTE AND CHOPPED

SALT AND PEPPER, TO TASTE

¾ LB. BUCATINI

½ CUP DRY WHITE WINE

2½ LBS. PLUM TOMATOES, PEELED, SEEDED, AND CHOPPED

2 PINCHES OF SUGAR

½ CUP GRATED PECORINO ROMANO CHEESE, PLUS MORE FOR GARNISH

1 HANDFUL OF FRESH PARSLEY, CHOPPED, FOR GARNISH

DIRECTIONS

1. Bring a large pot of water to a boil. Place the olive oil in a large, deep skillet and warm it over medium heat. When the oil starts to shimmer, add the guanciale or pancetta and the chilies and cook until the meat starts to brown, about 6 minutes. Transfer the meat to a small bowl and set it aside.

2. Add salt and the bucatini to the boiling water and cook the pasta 2 minutes less than the directed cooking time.

3. While the pasta is cooking, set the heat under the skillet to medium-high and add the wine. Scrape up all the browned bits stuck to bottom of the pan with a wooden spoon. Cook for 5 minutes, add the tomatoes and sugar, and season with salt and pepper. Cook for 10 minutes, adding a few spoonfuls of the pasta water if the sauce looks too thick.

4. Reserve ¼ cup of the pasta water and drain the pasta. Return the pot to the stove. Add the reserved pasta water, set the heat to high, add the pasta, drizzle it with olive oil, and toss for 1 minute. Transfer the pasta to skillet, sprinkle the Pecorino and guanciale or pancetta over it, and cook, tossing to distribute, for 2 minutes. Season the dish with salt and pepper and garnish it with parsley and additional Pecorino.

Orecchiette with Greens & Potatoes

YIELD: **4 SERVINGS**

ACTIVE TIME: **20 MINUTES**

TOTAL TIME: **30 MINUTES**

INGREDIENTS

6 TABLESPOONS OLIVE OIL, PLUS 1 TEASPOON

2 GARLIC CLOVES, HALVED

1 TEASPOON NONPAREIL CAPERS, RINSED, DRAINED, AND MINCED

½ CUP GREEN OLIVES, PITTED AND MINCED

⅛ TEASPOON CAYENNE PEPPER

2 LARGE RUSSET POTATOES, PEELED AND CHOPPED

SALT AND PEPPER, TO TASTE

¾ LB. ORECCHIETTE (SEE PAGE 32)

½ LB. GREENS

¼ CUP GRATED PECORINO ROMANO CHEESE, PLUS MORE FOR GARNISH

DIRECTIONS

1. Place 6 tablespoons of the olive oil in a large, deep skillet and warm it over low heat. When the oil starts to shimmer, add the garlic, capers, olives, and cayenne and sauté until the garlic starts to brown, about 3 minutes. Discard the garlic and remove the pan from heat.

2. Bring a pot of water to a boil and add the potatoes and salt. Boil for 6 minutes, add the pasta, and boil for 2 minutes. Add the greens 1 minute prior to draining the pasta. Reserve ½ cup of the pasta water, drain, and return the pot to the stove.

3. Set the skillet containing the sauce over medium-high heat. Add reserved pasta water to the pot, turn heat to high and add the pasta, potatoes, greens, and the remaining olive oil. Toss until the water has been absorbed. Transfer the mixture to the skillet and cook, tossing to combine, for 2 minutes. Add the Pecorino and toss until distributed. Season the dish with salt and pepper and garnish with additional Pecorino before serving.

Penne with Clams & Calamari

YIELD: **4 SERVINGS**

ACTIVE TIME: **25 MINUTES**

TOTAL TIME: **30 MINUTES**

INGREDIENTS

¾ LB. SQUID BODIES AND
TENTACLES, SLICED THIN

SALT AND PEPPER, TO TASTE

¼ CUP OLIVE OIL, PLUS 1
TEASPOON

3 LARGE PLUM TOMATOES, PEELED,
SEEDED, AND CHOPPED

2 GARLIC CLOVES, SLICED THIN

3½ LBS. SMALL HARD-SHELL
CLAMS, SCRUBBED AND RINSED

¾ LB. PENNE

2 HANDFULS OF FRESH PARSLEY,
CHOPPED

DIRECTIONS

1. Place the squid in a colander, rinse it, let it drain, and pat dry. Season with salt and pepper, toss, and set it aside.

2. Bring a large pot of water to a boil. Place the ¼ cup of olive oil in a large, deep skillet and warm it over medium-high heat. When the oil starts to shimmer, add the tomatoes and garlic, season with salt, and cook for 5 minutes. Add the squid and clams and cook, stirring occasionally, until a few of the clams open. Remove the pan from heat and cover it. Let it sit for 5 minutes, remove the cover, and discard any clams that did not open.

3. Add salt and the penne to the boiling water and cook 2 minutes less than the directed cooking time. Reserve ½ cup of the pasta water, drain the pasta, and return the pot to the stove. Raise the heat to high and add the remaining oil and the reserved pasta water. Add the pasta, toss to combine, and then add the contents of the skillet. Cook, tossing to distribute, for 2 minutes and garnish with the parsley before serving.

Kira's Garganelli

INGREDIENTS

1 TABLESPOON OLIVE OIL

6 OZ. UNSMOKED HAM, CUT INTO
1-INCH PIECES

4½ TABLESPOONS UNSALTED
BUTTER

3 SHALLOTS, MINCED

SALT AND WHITE PEPPER,
TO TASTE

¾ LB. GARGANELLI (SEE PAGE 38)

1½ CUPS FROZEN PEAS

¾ CUP HEAVY CREAM

1 TEASPOON FRESHLY GRATED
NUTMEG

PARMESAN CHEESE, GRATED,
FOR GARNISH

DIRECTIONS

1. Place the olive oil in a large, deep skillet and warm it over medium-high heat. When the oil starts to shimmer, add the ham and cook until it starts to brown, about 5 minutes. Transfer the ham to a small bowl and set it aside.

2. Add 4 tablespoons of the butter to the skillet and melt it over medium heat. Add the shallots and a pinch of salt and reduce the heat to low. Cover the pan and cook, stirring occasionally, until the shallots are very soft and golden brown, about 15 minutes.

3. While the shallots are cooking, bring a large pot of water to a boil. When it's boiling, add salt, the pasta, and peas and cook for 2 minutes. Drain the pasta and peas, reserving ½ cup of the cooking water beforehand.

4. Stir the cream and nutmeg into the skillet and season the mixture with salt and pepper. Bring to a simmer, cook for 3 minutes, and then remove the skillet from heat.

5. Return the pot to the stove. Add the remaining butter and reserved pasta water, raise the heat to high, add the drained pasta and peas, and toss to combine. Add the contents of the skillet and cook, tossing to combine, for 2 minutes. Top the dish with the ham and garnish with Parmesan.

Pasta Primavera

INGREDIENTS

6½ TABLESPOONS UNSALTED BUTTER

1 CUP PANKO

SALT AND PEPPER, TO TASTE

1 YELLOW BELL PEPPER, STEMMED, SEEDS AND RIBS REMOVED, AND SLICED

3 TABLESPOONS OLIVE OIL

2 CARROTS, PEELED AND SLICED THIN

1½ CUPS HEAVY CREAM

¼ TEASPOON WORCESTERSHIRE SAUCE

1 CUP PEAS

1½ CUPS GRATED PARMESAN CHEESE, PLUS MORE FOR GARNISH

1 TEASPOON FRESHLY GRATED NUTMEG

¾ LB. PASTA

1 CUP CHERRY TOMATOES, HALVED

2 HANDFULS OF FRESH PARSLEY, CHOPPED, FOR GARNISH

2 HANDFULS OF FRESH BASIL, CHOPPED, FOR GARNISH

DIRECTIONS

1. Preheat the oven to 400°F. Place 2 tablespoons of the butter in a large skillet and melt it over medium heat. Add the panko and cook, stirring constantly, until it is a dark golden brown, 4 to 5 minutes. Transfer the panko to a bowl, season with salt and pepper, and stir to combine.

2. Place the bell pepper in a large bowl, drizzle with 2 tablespoons of the oil, and toss until evenly coated. Transfer to a parchment-lined baking sheet and spread it out in a single layer. Add the carrots to the same large bowl, drizzle with the remaining oil, and toss until evenly coated. Transfer to another parchment-lined baking sheet and spread them out in a single layer. Place both baking sheets in the oven. Roast the pepper, stirring once about halfway through, until softened and browned, 10 to 12 minutes. Roast the carrots, stirring once about halfway through, until fork-tender and lightly browned, 15 to 18 minutes. Remove from the oven, season with salt and pepper, and set the vegetables aside.

3. While the vegetables are roasting, bring a large pot of water to a boil. Combine the cream, Worcestershire sauce, and 4 tablespoons of the butter in a medium saucepan and warm over medium-low heat until the butter melts. Gently stir in the peas and Parmesan, season with salt and pepper, and add the nutmeg. Bring to a gentle simmer and cook until the sauce thickens slightly, about 2 to 3 minutes. Remove from heat, cover the pan, and set it aside.

Continued...

4. Once the water is boiling, add salt and the pasta and cook 2 minutes short of the directed time. Reserve ¼ cup of pasta water, drain the pasta, and return the pot to the stove. Add reserved pasta water and the remaining butter, raise the heat to high, add the pasta, and cook, tossing to combine, until the water has been absorbed. Stir in the cherry tomatoes, the contents of the skillet, and the roasted vegetables and cook, while gently tossing to combine, for 2 minutes. Top the dish with the toasted panko and garnish with the parsley, basil, and additional Parmesan.

Spaghetti alla Carbonara

INGREDIENTS

2½ TABLESPOONS OLIVE OIL

4 OZ. BACON, DICED

SALT AND PEPPER, TO TASTE

2 LARGE EGGS, AT ROOM TEMPERATURE

¾ CUP GRATED PARMESAN CHEESE, PLUS MORE FOR GARNISH

1 LB. SPAGHETTI

DIRECTIONS

1. Bring a large saucepan of water to a boil. Add 2 tablespoons of the olive oil to a large skillet and warm it over medium heat. When the oil starts to shimmer, add the bacon, and season it with pepper. Sauté the bacon until its fat renders and it starts turning golden brown, about 5 minutes. Remove the skillet from heat and cover it partially.

2. Place the eggs in a small bowl and whisk until scrambled. Add the Parmesan, season with salt and pepper, and stir until combined.

3. Add salt and the pasta to the boiling water. Cook 2 minutes short of the directed cooking time, reserve ¼ cup of the pasta water, and drain the pasta. Return the pot to the stove, raise the heat to high, and add the remaining olive oil and the reserved pasta water. Add the drained pasta and toss to combine. Cook until the pasta has absorbed the water. Remove the pot from heat, add the bacon and the egg-and-Parmesan mixture, and toss to coat the pasta. Divide the pasta between the serving bowls, season with pepper, and top each portion with additional Parmesan.

Mac & Cheese with Browned Butter Bread Crumbs

YIELD: **6 SERVINGS**

ACTIVE TIME: **30 MINUTES**

TOTAL TIME: **1 HOUR**

INGREDIENTS

SALT, TO TASTE

1 LB. ELBOW MACARONI

7 TABLESPOONS UNSALTED BUTTER

2 CUPS PANKO

½ YELLOW ONION, MINCED

3 TABLESPOONS ALL-PURPOSE FLOUR

1 TABLESPOON YELLOW MUSTARD

1 TEASPOON TURMERIC

1 TEASPOON GARLIC POWDER

1 TEASPOON WHITE PEPPER

2 CUPS LIGHT CREAM

2 CUPS WHOLE MILK

1 LB. AMERICAN CHEESE, SLICED

10 OZ. BOURSIN CHEESE

½ LB. EXTRA-SHARP CHEDDAR CHEESE, SLICED

DIRECTIONS

1. Preheat the oven to 400°F. Fill a Dutch oven with water and bring it to a boil. Add salt and the macaroni and cook until the macaroni is just shy of al dente, about 7 minutes. Drain and set aside.

2. Place the pot over medium heat and add 3 tablespoons of the butter. Cook until the butter starts to give off a nutty smell and brown. Add the panko, stir, and cook until it starts to look like wet sand, about 4 minutes. Remove the panko from the pan and set it aside.

3. Wipe out the Dutch oven, place it over medium-high heat, and add the onion and the remaining butter. Sauté until the onion is soft, about 10 minutes. Gradually add the flour, stirring constantly to prevent lumps from forming. Add the mustard, turmeric, garlic powder, and white pepper and stir until combined. Stir in the light cream and the milk, reduce the heat to medium, and bring the mixture to a simmer.

4. Add the cheeses one at a time, stirring to incorporate before adding the next one. When all of the cheeses have been incorporated and the mixture is smooth, cook until the flour taste is gone, about 10 minutes. Stir in the macaroni and top with the panko.

5. Place the Dutch oven in the oven and bake until the panko is crispy, 10 to 15 minutes. Remove from the oven and serve immediately.

YIELD: **6 SERVINGS**

ACTIVE TIME: **40 MINUTES**

TOTAL TIME: **1 HOUR**

Spaghetti & Meatballs

INGREDIENTS

2 TABLESPOONS OLIVE OIL

1 SMALL ONION, MINCED

3 GARLIC CLOVES, MINCED

¼ TEASPOON RED PEPPER FLAKES

1 LARGE EGG

2 TABLESPOONS WHOLE MILK

½ CUP ITALIAN BREAD CRUMBS

¼ CUP GRATED PARMESAN CHEESE

¼ CUP GRATED FRESH
MOZZARELLA CHEESE

2 TABLESPOONS FINELY CHOPPED
FRESH PARSLEY

1 TEASPOON ITALIAN SEASONING

½ LB. GROUND PORK

½ LB. GROUND CHUCK

¼ LB. GROUND VEAL

SALT AND PEPPER, TO TASTE

1 LB. SPAGHETTI

2 CUPS MARINARA SAUCE
(SEE PAGE 67)

DIRECTIONS

1. Preheat the broiler to high, position a rack so that the tops of the meatballs will be approximately 6 inches below the broiler, and line a rimmed baking sheet with aluminum foil.

2. Place the oil in a large skillet and warm over medium-high heat. When it starts to shimmer, add the onion, garlic, and red pepper flakes and sauté until the onion is translucent, about 3 minutes. Remove the pan from heat and set it aside.

3. Place the egg, milk, bread crumbs, Parmesan, mozzarella, parsley, and Italian seasoning in a mixing bowl and stir until combined. Add the pork, beef, veal, and the onion mixture, season with salt and pepper, and stir until thoroughly combined. Working with wet hands, form the mixture into 1½-inch meatballs, arrange them on the baking sheet, and spray the tops with cooking spray.

4. Place the meatballs in the oven and broil until browned all over, turning them as they cook. Remove the meatballs from the oven and set them aside.

5. While the meatballs are in the oven, bring water to a boil in a large saucepan. Add salt and the spaghetti and cook until the pasta is al dente, about 8 minutes.

6. Place the sauce in the skillet and warm it over medium heat. Add the meatballs to the sauce, reduce the heat to low, cover the pan, and simmer, turning the meatballs occasionally, until they are cooked through, about 15 minutes.

7. Drain the pasta and divide it between the serving plates. Ladle the sauce and meatballs over the top and serve.

YIELD: **6 SERVINGS**

ACTIVE TIME: **40 MINUTES**

TOTAL TIME: **1 HOUR**

Penne alla Vodka

INGREDIENTS

2½ TABLESPOONS UNSALTED BUTTER

4 OZ. PANCETTA, DICED

3 SHALLOTS, MINCED

SALT, TO TASTE

1 (28 OZ.) CAN OF PEELED WHOLE SAN MARZANO TOMATOES, PUREED

1 TEASPOON RED PEPPER FLAKES

1 CUP HEAVY CREAM

1¼ LBS. PENNE

½ CUP VODKA, AT ROOM TEMPERATURE

1 CUP GRATED PARMESAN CHEESE, PLUS MORE FOR GARNISH

2 HANDFULS OF FRESH PARSLEY, CHOPPED, FOR GARNISH

DIRECTIONS

1. Place 2 tablespoons of the butter in a large skillet and melt it over medium heat. Add the pancetta and sauté until the pieces are browned and crispy, about 6 minutes. Transfer to a small bowl and set aside. Add the shallots and a pinch of salt, reduce the heat to low, cover the pan, and cook, stirring occasionally, until the shallots are soft, about 10 minutes.

2. Add the tomatoes and red pepper flakes to the skillet, season with salt, and raise the heat to medium-high. Once the mixture begins to boil, reduce the heat to low, partially cover the pan, and cook until the sauce thickens slightly, 15 to 20 minutes. Add the cream and heat through until the sauce gently bubbles. Remove from heat and cover the pan.

3. Bring a pot of water to a boil, add salt and the pasta, and cook 2 minutes short of the directed time. Reserve ¼ cup of pasta water, drain, and return the pot to the stove. Add the reserved pasta water and remaining butter, turn heat to high, add the pasta, and cook, tossing to combine, until the pasta has absorbed the water. Add the sauce and the Parmesan to the pot and toss to combine. Top the dish with the pancetta and garnish with the parsley and additional Parmesan.

YIELD: **6 SERVINGS**

ACTIVE TIME: **20 MINUTES**

TOTAL TIME: **40 MINUTES**

Sweet Potato Gnocchi with Sage Brown Butter

INGREDIENTS

SWEET POTATO GNOCCHI (SEE PAGE 48)

1 STICK OF UNSALTED BUTTER

1 TABLESPOON FINELY CHOPPED FRESH SAGE

2 CUPS ARUGULA

½ CUP WALNUTS, TOASTED AND CHOPPED

DIRECTIONS

1. Bring a large pot of water to a boil. Working in small batches, add the gnocchi to the boiling water and stir to keep them from sticking to the bottom. The gnocchi will eventually float to the surface. Cook for 1 more minute, remove, and transfer to the bowl containing the olive oil. Toss to coat and transfer to a parchment-lined baking sheet to cool.

2. Place the butter in a skillet and warm over medium heat until it begins to brown. Add the sage and cook until butter stops foaming. Place the arugula in a bowl and set it aside.

3. Working in batches, add the gnocchi to the skillet, stir to coat, and cook until they have a nice sear on one side. Transfer to the bowl of arugula and toss to combine. Serve and top each portion with the toasted walnuts.

Tagliatelle with Asparagus & Peas

INGREDIENTS

SALT, TO TASTE

1 BUNCH OF ASPARAGUS, TRIMMED AND CHOPPED

½ LB. SNAP PEAS, TRIMMED AND CHOPPED

¾ LB. TAGLIATELLE (SEE PAGE 20 FOR HOMEMADE)

4 TABLESPOONS UNSALTED BUTTER

¼ CUP GRATED PARMESAN CHEESE

½ TEASPOON RED PEPPER FLAKES

DIRECTIONS

1. Bring water to a boil in a medium saucepan and also in a large saucepan. Add salt to each of the saucepans once the water is boiling. Place the asparagus and peas in the medium saucepan and cook for 1 minute. Drain and set aside.

2. Place the pasta in the large saucepan and cook for 3 minutes, stirring constantly. Reserve ¼ cup of the pasta water and then drain the pasta.

3. Place the butter in a large skillet and melt over medium heat. Add the pasta and vegetables and toss to combine. Add the reserved pasta water, Parmesan, and red pepper flakes and toss to evenly coat. Season to taste and serve.

Butternut Squash Cannelloni

YIELD: **8 SERVINGS**

ACTIVE TIME: **1 HOUR**

TOTAL TIME: **1 HOUR AND 30 MINUTES**

INGREDIENTS

FOR THE FILLING

2 LBS. BUTTERNUT SQUASH, HALVED AND SEEDED

3 TABLESPOONS OLIVE OIL

5 GARLIC CLOVES, MINCED

1½ CUPS RICOTTA CHEESE

1 CUP GRATED PARMESAN CHEESE

12 FRESH SAGE LEAVES, SLICED THIN

1 TEASPOON FRESHLY GRATED NUTMEG

SALT AND WHITE PEPPER, TO TASTE

FOR THE PASTA

ALL-YOLK PASTA DOUGH (SEE PAGE 22)

SEMOLINA FLOUR, FOR DUSTING

SALT, TO TASTE

½ TABLESPOON OLIVE OIL, PLUS MORE AS NEEDED

DIRECTIONS

1. To begin preparations for the filling, preheat the oven to 375°F. Brush the flesh of the squash with 1 tablespoon of the olive oil and place the squash on a parchment-lined baking sheet, cut side down. Place the baking sheet in the oven and roast until the squash is fork-tender, 40 to 45 minutes. Remove the squash from the oven and let it cool. When it is cool enough to handle, scoop the flesh into a wide, shallow bowl and mash it until it is smooth.

2. Place the remaining olive oil in a large skillet and warm over medium heat. When the oil starts to shimmer, add the garlic and sauté for 1 minute. Remove the pan from heat and transfer the garlic and oil to the bowl with the mashed squash. Add the cheeses, half of the sage, the nutmeg, season the mixture with salt and pepper, and stir to combine.

3. To begin preparations for the pasta, run the dough through a pasta maker until the sheets are about 1⁄16 inch thick. Lay the sheets on lightly floured, parchment paper–lined baking sheets. Working with one sheet at a time, place it on a flour-dusted work surface in front of you. Using a pastry cutter, cut each sheet into as many 4½- to 5-inch squares as possible. Place the finished squares on another flour-dusted, parchment-lined baking sheet so they don't touch. As you run out of room, lightly dust the squares with flour, cover with another sheet of parchment, and arrange more squares on top of that. Repeat with all the pasta sheets. Gather any scraps together into a ball, put it through the pasta maker to create additional pasta sheets, and cut those as well.

Continued...

4. Bring a large pot of water to a boil. Once it's boiling, add salt and stir to dissolve. Add the squares and cook until they are just tender, about 2 minutes. Drain, rinse under cold water, and toss with a teaspoon of olive oil to keep them from sticking together.

5. Generously coat a baking dish large enough to fit all the filled cannelloni in a single layer with olive oil. To fill the cannelloni, place a pasta square in front of you. Place ¼ cup of the squash mixture in the center of the square and shape it into a rough cylinder. Roll the pasta square around the filling and transfer it to the prepared baking dish, seam side down. Repeat with remaining sheets and filling. When the baking dish is filled, brush the tops of the cannelloni with the remaining olive oil.

6. Preheat the oven to 375°F and place a rack in the center position. Put the baking dish in the oven and bake until the cannelloni are very hot and begin to turn golden brown, about 20 minutes. Top with the remaining sage and serve.

Classic Lasagna

INGREDIENTS

ALL-YOLK PASTA DOUGH (SEE PAGE 22)

1 TABLESPOON SALT, PLUS MORE TO TASTE

1½ LBS. RICOTTA CHEESE

2 EGGS

1½ CUPS SHREDDED ITALIAN CHEESE BLEND (EQUAL PARTS ASIAGO, FONTINA, MOZZARELLA, PROVOLONE, PARMESAN, AND ROMANO), PLUS MORE FOR TOPPING

½ TEASPOON BLACK PEPPER

½ TEASPOON ONION POWDER

½ TEASPOON GARLIC POWDER

PINCH OF FRESHLY GRATED NUTMEG

1 TABLESPOON FINELY CHOPPED FRESH BASIL

1 TEASPOON DRIED OREGANO

½ CUP CHOPPED FRESH PARSLEY

2 CUPS BOLOGNESE SAUCE (SEE PAGE 88), PLUS MORE AS NEEDED

DIRECTIONS

1. Preheat the oven to 350°F. Divide the dough into four pieces and run them through a pasta maker until they are ¹⁄₁₆ inch thick. Cut the pieces into 14-inch-long sheets and place them on a flour-dusted, parchment-lined baking sheet. Gather any scraps into a ball, run this through the pasta maker, and cut into additional lasagna sheets.

2. Place all of the remaining ingredients in a mixing bowl and stir to combine.

3. Cover the bottom of a 9 x 13–inch baking dish with sauce. Place a layer of lasagna noodles on top and cover them with one-third of the bolognese-and-cheese mixture. Alternate layers of the noodles and the mixture until all of the mixture has been used up. Top with another layer of noodles and spread a thin layer of sauce over them.

4. Place the dish in the oven and bake for 45 minutes. Remove from the oven, sprinkle more of the cheese blend on top, and return to the oven. Bake until the cheese has melted and is starting to brown, about 5 minutes. Remove the lasagna from the oven and let it stand for 20 minutes before slicing and serving.

Porcini Mushroom & Béchamel Lasagna

YIELD: **6 SERVINGS**

ACTIVE TIME: **1 HOUR**

TOTAL TIME: **2 HOURS**

INGREDIENTS

1 CUP DRY RED WINE

ALL-YOLK PASTA DOUGH (SEE PAGE 22)

2 TABLESPOONS UNSALTED BUTTER

3 SHALLOTS, MINCED

SALT AND PEPPER, TO TASTE

2 GARLIC CLOVES, MINCED

1 LB. CREMINI MUSHROOMS, STEMMED AND SLICED THIN

1 OZ. DRIED PORCINI MUSHROOMS, RECONSTITUTED AND CHOPPED, SOAKING LIQUID RESERVED

BÉCHAMEL SAUCE (SEE PAGE 103)

2 TABLESPOONS FINELY CHOPPED FRESH THYME, PLUS MORE FOR GARNISH

1½ CUPS GRATED PARMESAN CHEESE

DIRECTIONS

1. Place the wine in a small saucepan and bring it to a boil. Cook until it has reduced almost by half, about 5 minutes. Remove the pan from heat and set it aside.

2. Preheat the oven to 350°F. Divide the dough into four pieces and run them through a pasta maker until they are ⅟₁₆ inch thick. Cut the pieces into 14-inch-long sheets and place them on a flour-dusted, parchment-lined baking sheet. Gather any scraps into a ball, run this through the pasta maker, and cut into additional lasagna sheets.

3. Place the butter in a large, deep skillet and melt it over medium heat. Add the shallots and a pinch of salt and sauté until the shallots are translucent, about 3 minutes. Reduce the temperature to low, cover the pan, and cook, stirring occasionally, until the shallots have softened, about 10 minutes. Stir in the garlic and sauté for 30 seconds.

4. Raise the heat to medium-high, add the cremini and porcini mushrooms, season with salt, and cook, while stirring frequently, until the mushrooms begin to release their liquid, about 5 minutes. Add the reduced wine and the porcini soaking liquid and bring to a gentle simmer. Cook, stirring occasionally, until the mushrooms are tender and the liquid has reduced by half, 12 to 15 minutes. Remove from the heat, season to taste, and then stir in the Béchamel Sauce and thyme.

Continued...

5. Cover the bottom of a deep 9 x 13-inch baking pan with some of the mushroom mixture. Cover with a layer of noodles, making sure they are slightly overlapping. Cover with a layer of the mushroom mixture and sprinkle ½ cup of the Parmesan on top. Repeat this layering two more times, concluding with a layer of the mushroom mixture topped with the remaining Parmesan. Cover the pan loosely with aluminum foil, place in the oven, and bake for 35 minutes. Remove the foil and continue to bake until the edges of the lasagna sheets are lightly browned, about 12 minutes. For nice, clean slices, remove the lasagna from the oven and allow it to rest for at least 20 minutes before slicing.

Pici with Crispy Anchovy Bread Crumbs

INGREDIENTS

⅓ CUP OLIVE OIL, PLUS 2½ TABLESPOONS

10 ANCHOVY FILLETS IN OLIVE OIL

2 CUPS BREAD CRUMBS

SALT AND PEPPER, TO TASTE

¾ LB. PICI

2 HANDFULS OF FRESH PARSLEY, CHOPPED, FOR GARNISH

DIRECTIONS

1. Bring a large pot of water to a boil. Place the ⅓ cup of olive oil in a large skillet and warm over medium heat. When the oil starts to shimmer, add the anchovy fillets, mash them with a fork, and cook until they disintegrate, about 3 minutes.

2. Raise the heat to medium-high and stir in the bread crumbs. Cook until they are golden brown, about 3 minutes, and remove the skillet from heat. Season the mixture with salt and pepper and set it aside.

3. Add salt and the pasta to the boiling water and cook for 2 minutes less than the pasta's directed cooking time. Reserve ½ cup of the cooking water, drain, return the empty pot to the stove, and raise the heat to high. Add the remaining oil and reserved pasta water and stir to combine. Add the drained pasta and cook, tossing continuously, for 2 minutes. Transfer the pasta to a warm bowl. Top with the warm anchovy-and-bread crumb mixture, toss to combine, and garnish with the parsley.

TIP: For best results, use day-old bread that is not rock hard to make the bread crumbs.

YIELD: **4 SERVINGS**

ACTIVE TIME: **15 MINUTES**

TOTAL TIME: **20 MINUTES**

Fettuccine Alfredo

INGREDIENTS

SALT AND PEPPER, TO TASTE

¾ LB. FETTUCCINE (SEE PAGE 20 FOR HOMEMADE)

½ CUP HEAVY CREAM

2½ TABLESPOONS UNSALTED BUTTER, AT ROOM TEMPERATURE

1 CUP GRATED PARMESAN CHEESE, PLUS MORE FOR GARNISH

½ TEASPOON FRESHLY GRATED NUTMEG

DIRECTIONS

1. Bring a large pot of water to a boil. Once it's boiling, add salt and the pasta and cook for 2 minutes. Reserve ½ cup of pasta water and drain the pasta.

2. Place the reserved pasta water and heavy cream in a large skillet and bring it to a simmer. Add the butter and stir until it has been emulsified. Gradually incorporate the Parmesan, making sure each addition has melted before adding the next.

3. Add the pasta to the skillet and toss to combine. Sprinkle the nutmeg over the top before serving.

Pasta con le Sarde

INGREDIENTS

1½ LB. SARDINE FILLETS

½ CUP GOLDEN RAISINS

⅓ CUP PINE NUTS

SALT AND PEPPER, TO TASTE

1 HANDFUL OF FENNEL FRONDS

5 TABLESPOONS OLIVE OIL, PLUS
MORE AS NEEDED

1 SMALL YELLOW ONION, HALVED
AND SLICED THIN

5 ANCHOVY FILLETS IN OLIVE OIL,
CHOPPED

½ TEASPOON FENNEL SEEDS

¾ LB. SPAGHETTI

DIRECTIONS

1. Wash the sardine fillets under cold water and pat them dry with paper towels. Chop half of the fillets into 1-inch pieces and leave the remainder whole.

2. Place the raisins in a small bowl, cover them with warm water, and soak for 10 minutes. Drain and transfer to a paper towel–lined plate to dry.

3. Warm a small skillet over medium-low heat for 2 minutes. Add the pine nuts and cook, stirring frequently, for 3 to 4 minutes. Remove the pan from heat and season the pine nuts with salt. Set them aside.

4. Bring a large pot of water to a boil. When it's boiling, add the fennel fronds and boil for 1 minute. Remove them from the water using a strainer, drain well, pat dry with paper towels, and chop. Keep the water at a low simmer.

5. Add 3 tablespoons of the olive oil to a large skillet and warm it over medium heat. When the oil begins to shimmer, add the onion and a couple pinches of salt and sauté until the onion is soft, about 10 minutes. Add the raisins and pine nuts, sauté for another 3 minutes, and then stir in the blanched fennel fronds and a pinch of salt. Reduce the heat to low, cover, and cook, stirring occasionally, until the onion becomes very tender, about 15 minutes. If the mixture begins to look too dry, add a tablespoon or two of the simmering water.

Continued...

6. Preheat the oven to 400°F and oil a deep 9 x 13-inch baking dish. Add the anchovies, chopped sardines, and fennel seeds to the skillet with the onion mixture and cook, stirring frequently, until the anchovies have completely dissolved, about 10 minutes.

7. Return the water to a boil. Once it's boiling, add salt and the spaghetti and cook 2 minutes less than the directed cooking time. Reserve ¼ cup of the pasta water and drain the spaghetti. Transfer the pasta to the skillet, add the reserved pasta water, and toss to combine. Transfer the mixture to the prepared baking dish, top it with the whole sardine fillets, drizzle the remaining 2 tablespoons oil over it, and season with pepper. Place it in the oven and bake until the sardines start to brown, about 15 minutes. Remove from the oven and let cool slightly before serving.

Baked Shells with Zucchini, Ham, and Béchamel Sauce

YIELD: **6 SERVINGS**

ACTIVE TIME: **1 HOUR**

TOTAL TIME: **1 HOUR AND 45 MINUTES**

INGREDIENTS

2 TABLESPOONS OLIVE OIL

1 YELLOW ONION, CHOPPED

SALT AND PEPPER, TO TASTE

3 ZUCCHINI, MINCED

¾ LB. LARGE SHELL PASTA

¼ CUP BREAD CRUMBS

½ LB. FRESH MOZZARELLA CHEESE, GRATED

½ LB. HONEY HAM, MINCED

BÉCHAMEL SAUCE (SEE PAGE 103)

1½ CUPS GRATED PARMESAN CHEESE

DIRECTIONS

1. Place the olive oil in a large skillet and warm it over medium heat. When the oil begins to shimmer, add the onion and a couple pinches of salt and sauté until the onion is soft, about 10 minutes. Add the zucchini and sauté until it is cooked through, about 10 minutes. Remove the pan from heat and let the mixture cool.

2. Bring a large pot of water to a boil. Once it's boiling, add salt and the pasta and cook for three-quarters of the directed time. Drain, rinse under cold water, and place the shells on paper towels to dry.

3. Preheat the oven to 375°F. Combine the zucchini mixture, bread crumbs, mozzarella, ham, and 1 cup of the Béchamel Sauce in a large bowl, season to taste, and gently stir until combined. Divide the mixture between the cooked shells. Spread ¾ cup of the Béchamel Sauce over the bottom of a baking dish large enough to accommodate the pasta in a single layer. Add the filled shells and pour the remaining Béchamel Sauce over the top. Sprinkle the Parmesan over the top and cover the dish with aluminum foil.

4. Place the dish in the oven and reduce the temperature to 350°F. Bake for 20 minutes, remove the foil, and bake until the tops of the shells just start to turn golden brown, about 10 minutes. Remove from the oven and let cool briefly before serving.

Baked Ziti

INGREDIENTS

2 TABLESPOONS OLIVE OIL

½ CUP DICED PANCETTA

1 LARGE YELLOW ONION, CHOPPED

SALT AND PEPPER, TO TASTE

2 TEASPOONS RED PEPPER FLAKES

1 TABLESPOON TOMATO PASTE

1 TABLESPOON FISH SAUCE

3 (14 OZ.) CANS OF PEELED WHOLE SAN MARZANO TOMATOES, WITH THEIR LIQUID, PUREED

¼ TEASPOON SUGAR

1½ TABLESPOONS UNSALTED BUTTER

1 CUP BÉCHAMEL SAUCE (SEE PAGE 103)

1 LB. FRESH MOZZARELLA CHEESE, CHOPPED

1 LB. ZITI

2½ CUPS GRATED PARMESAN CHEESE

1 HANDFUL OF FRESH BASIL, CHOPPED, FOR GARNISH

DIRECTIONS

1. Place the olive oil in a large skillet and warm it over medium heat. When the oil begins to shimmer, add the pancetta and sauté until it is golden brown, 4 to 5 minutes. Raise the heat to medium-high and add the onion, a couple pinches of salt, and the red pepper flakes. Reduce the heat to low, cover the pan, and cook, stirring occasionally, until the onion has become very soft, about 15 minutes.

2. Raise the heat to medium-high, stir in the tomato paste and fish sauce, and cook, stirring constantly, until the mixture has slightly darkened, about 2 minutes. Stir in the tomatoes, sugar, and a couple pinches of salt and bring the sauce to a gentle boil. Reduce the heat to low and cook, stirring frequently, until the sauce has slightly reduced, about 30 minutes. Season to taste with salt and pepper.

3. Preheat the oven to 350°F. Butter the sides and bottom of 9 x 13–inch baking dish. Combine the Béchamel Sauce and the mozzarella in a large bowl. Bring a large pot of water to a boil. Once it's boiling, add salt and the pasta and cook for half of the directed time. Drain and immediately add the pasta to the bowl containing the Béchamel Sauce-and-mozzarella mixture. Add 1 cup of the Parmesan and toss to combine.

4. Add all but 1½ cups of the tomato sauce to the bowl and gently fold to incorporate. Transfer the mixture to the baking dish and top with the remaining tomato sauce and Parmesan. Bake for 15 to 20 minutes and then turn the broiler on and broil the dish until the top starts to brown, about 4 minutes. Remove from the oven and let the dish rest for 15 minutes before serving. Garnish each portion with some of the basil.

Pastitsio

INGREDIENTS

2 TABLESPOONS OLIVE OIL

2 ONIONS, MINCED

SALT AND PEPPER, TO TASTE

4 LARGE GARLIC CLOVES, MINCED

2 LBS. GROUND LAMB

2 CUPS WHOLE MILK

1 (28 OZ.) CAN OF PUREED TOMATOES

4 SPRIGS OF FRESH THYME

1 TABLESPOON FRESHLY GRATED NUTMEG

1 TEASPOON CINNAMON

BUTTER, AS NEEDED

BÉCHAMEL SAUCE (SEE PAGE 103)

1 LB. ZITI

1⅔ CUPS GRATED PARMESAN CHEESE

1 CUP PANKO

DIRECTIONS

1. Place the olive oil in a large, deep skillet and warm it over medium heat. When the oil starts to shimmer, add the onions and a couple pinches of salt, reduce the heat to low, cover the pan, and cook, stirring occasionally, for about 20 minutes.

2. Add the garlic, sauté for 1 minute, raise the heat to medium-high, and add the lamb, breaking it up with a fork as it browns. When the lamb is brown and cooked through, stir in the milk and cook until all of the liquid has evaporated, about 15 minutes.

3. Add the tomatoes, thyme, nutmeg, and cinnamon, season with salt and pepper, and bring the mixture to a boil. Reduce the heat to low, cover the pan, and cook, stirring occasionally, for 2 hours. If the sauce looks too watery after 1½ hours of cooking, let it cook uncovered for the last half hour. Discard the thyme and set the mixture aside.

4. Preheat the oven to 400°F. Butter the bottom and sides of a 9 x 13-inch baking dish with the butter and bring a large pot of water to a boil. Once it's boiling, add salt and the ziti and cook the pasta for three-quarters of the directed time. Drain, transfer to the prepared baking dish along with 2 cups of the Béchamel Sauce, and toss to coat. Arrange the ziti so that they are all lined up side by side.

Continued…

5. Reduce the oven temperature to 375°F. Place the baking dish in the oven and bake until the sauce is bubbling, 40 to 45 minutes.

6. While the dish is in the oven, reheat the meat sauce. Toss the Parmesan and panko together in a medium bowl. Remove the dish from the oven and sprinkle the panko-and-cheese mixture evenly over the top. Return the dish to the oven and turn on the broiler. Remove the dish when the topping turns golden brown and let cool for 15 minutes before slicing. To serve, ladle the meat sauce into the bottom of a warmed bowl and then top with a slice of the Pastitsio.

CHAPTER 5

OVER THE TOP

---

*Yes, a decadent slice of lasagna or a pile of pillowy gnocchi
are difficult to outdo. But at the end of day, it is pasta's abilities in a
supporting role that really allow it to shine. By doing nothing more than
simply arranging some delicacy such as Eggplant Parmesan (see page 211)
atop a pile of handmade noodles, you can all but guarantee that you'll
see nothing but smiles when you glance around the dinner table.*

Slow Cooker Cacciatore

INGREDIENTS

6 BONELESS, SKINLESS CHICKEN THIGHS

1 (28 OZ.) CAN OF WHOLE SAN MARZANO TOMATOES, DRAINED

1 (28 OZ.) CAN OF DICED TOMATOES, WITH THEIR JUICE

⅔ CUP DRY RED WINE

4 SHALLOTS, CHOPPED

3 GARLIC CLOVES, MINCED

1 GREEN BELL PEPPER, STEMMED, SEEDS AND RIBS REMOVED, AND CHOPPED

1 YELLOW BELL PEPPER, STEMMED, SEEDS AND RIBS REMOVED, AND CHOPPED

1 CUP BUTTON MUSHROOM CAPS, CHOPPED

1½ TEASPOONS DRIED OREGANO

1 TABLESPOON GARLIC POWDER

1 TABLESPOON SUGAR

2 TABLESPOONS KOSHER SALT, PLUS MORE TO TASTE

½ TEASPOON RED PEPPER FLAKES

BLACK PEPPER, TO TASTE

PARMESAN CHEESE, GRATED, FOR GARNISH

FRESH PARSLEY, FINELY CHOPPED, FOR GARNISH

DIRECTIONS

1. Place all of the ingredients, save the Parmesan and parsley, in a slow cooker and cook on low until the chicken is very tender, about 5½ hours. The cooking time may vary depending on your slow cooker, so be sure to check after about 4½ hours to avoid overcooking.

2. To serve, top each portion with a generous amount of Parmesan cheese and parsley.

Garlic & Basil Baked Cod

INGREDIENTS

2 LBS. COD FILLETS

SALT AND PEPPER, TO TASTE

2 TABLESPOONS FINELY CHOPPED FRESH OREGANO

1 TEASPOON CORIANDER

1 TEASPOON PAPRIKA

10 GARLIC CLOVES, MINCED

15 FRESH BASIL LEAVES, SHREDDED

6 TABLESPOONS OLIVE OIL

2 TABLESPOONS FRESH LEMON JUICE

2 SHALLOTS, SLICED

2 TOMATOES, SLICED

DIRECTIONS

1. Place the cod in a mixing bowl or a large resealable plastic bag and add the remaining ingredients, except for the shallots and tomatoes. Stir to combine, place the mixture in the refrigerator, and let the cod marinate for 1 hour, stirring or shaking occasionally.

2. Preheat the oven to 425°F, remove the cod from the refrigerator, and let it come to room temperature. Cover the bottom of a baking dish with the shallots, place the cod on top, and top the fish with the tomatoes. Pour the marinade over the mixture, place it in the oven, and bake for about 15 minutes, until the fish is flaky. Remove from the oven and let it rest briefly before serving.

Baked Salmon with Cilantro-Garlic Sauce

YIELD: **4 SERVINGS**

ACTIVE TIME: **10 MINUTES**

TOTAL TIME: **25 MINUTES**

INGREDIENTS

2 LBS. SALMON FILLETS, BONED

SALT AND PEPPER, TO TASTE

6 GARLIC CLOVES

1 BUNCH OF FRESH CILANTRO, CHOPPED

½ CUP OLIVE OIL, PLUS MORE AS NEEDED

2 TABLESPOONS FRESH LIME JUICE

2 TOMATOES, SLICED

1 LIME, SLICED

DIRECTIONS

1. Preheat the oven to 425°F. Season the salmon with salt and pepper and let it rest at room temperature as the oven warms up.

2. Place the garlic, cilantro, olive oil, lime juice, and a pinch of salt in a food processor and blitz until pureed.

3. Oil a baking dish and place the salmon in it. Spoon the garlic-and-cilantro puree over the salmon and then top it with the slices of tomato and lime.

4. Place the salmon in the oven and bake until the interior of each fillet is 125°F, about 8 minutes. Remove from the oven, cover the dish with aluminum foil, and let it rest for 8 minutes. Serve with any remaining puree on the side.

NOTE: The cooking time assumes that the fillets are each about 1 inch thick. If they are thinner or thicker, adjust the cooking time accordingly.

Garlic & Lime Calamari

YIELD: **4 SERVINGS**

ACTIVE TIME: **10 MINUTES**

TOTAL TIME: **20 MINUTES**

INGREDIENTS

1½ LBS. SQUID, SLICED

2 TABLESPOONS OLIVE OIL

1 TABLESPOON UNSALTED BUTTER

10 GARLIC CLOVES, CHOPPED

3 TABLESPOONS WHITE WINE

JUICE OF 1½ LIMES

SALT AND PEPPER, TO TASTE

PINCH OF CAYENNE PEPPER

2 TABLESPOONS FINELY CHOPPED
FRESH DILL

DIRECTIONS

1. Pat the calamari dry and set it aside. Place the olive oil and butter in a large cast-iron skillet and warm over medium-high heat. When the butter has melted, add the garlic and sauté until fragrant, about 1 minute.

2. Add the calamari to the pan, cook for 2 minutes, and then stir in the wine and lime juice. Cook for another 30 seconds, until warmed through, and remove the pan from heat. Season with salt and pepper, stir in the cayenne and dill, and serve.

Stuffed Eggplants

YIELD: **4 SERVINGS**

ACTIVE TIME: **30 MINUTES**

TOTAL TIME: **1 HOUR AND 20 MINUTES**

INGREDIENTS

2 LARGE EGGPLANTS, HALVED

2 TABLESPOONS OLIVE OIL, PLUS MORE AS NEEDED

½ CUP QUINOA, RINSED

1 CUP WATER

2 ONIONS, CHOPPED

3 GARLIC CLOVES, MINCED

2 BELL PEPPERS, STEMMED, SEEDS AND RIBS REMOVED, AND CHOPPED

1 LB. GROUND LAMB

SALT AND PEPPER, TO TASTE

½ TEASPOON GARAM MASALA

2 TEASPOONS CUMIN

FRESH PARSLEY, FINELY CHOPPED, FOR GARNISH

DIRECTIONS

1. Preheat the oven to 400°F. Place the eggplants on a baking sheet, drizzle olive oil over the top, and place them in the oven. Roast until the flesh is tender, about 30 minutes. Remove from the oven and let the eggplants cool slightly. When cool enough to handle, scoop out the flesh, mince it, and place it in a mixing bowl. Set the hollowed-out eggplants aside and leave the oven on.

2. Place the quinoa and water in a saucepan and bring to a boil over medium heat. Let the quinoa boil until it has absorbed all of the water. Remove the pan from heat, cover it, and let it steam for 5 minutes. Fluff with a fork and let cool slightly.

3. Place the olive oil in a large skillet and warm it over medium-high heat. When the oil starts to shimmer, add the onions, garlic, and bell peppers and sauté until the onions and peppers start to soften, about 5 minutes. Add the ground lamb, season it with salt and pepper, stir in the garam masala and cumin, and cook, breaking the lamb up with a fork, until it is browned, about 6 minutes. Transfer the mixture to the bowl containing the minced eggplant. Add the quinoa to the bowl and stir until the mixture is combined.

4. Fill the cavities of the hollowed-out eggplants with the lamb-and-quinoa mixture. Place them on a baking sheet, place them in the oven, and roast until the eggplants are starting to collapse, about 15 minutes. Remove from the oven and let them cool slightly before garnishing with the parsley and serving.

Pesto Chicken with Charred Tomatoes

YIELD: **4 SERVINGS**

ACTIVE TIME: **5 MINUTES**

TOTAL TIME: **3 HOURS AND 30 MINUTES**

INGREDIENTS

2 LBS. BONE-IN, SKIN-ON CHICKEN PIECES

SALT AND PEPPER, TO TASTE

2 BATCHES OF BASIL PESTO (SEE PAGE 71)

4 PLUM TOMATOES, HALVED

DIRECTIONS

1. Season the chicken with salt and pepper. Place the pesto in a bowl, add the chicken pieces, and stir until they are evenly coated. Cover the bowl and let the chicken marinate in the refrigerator for 2 hours.

2. Preheat the oven to 400°F. Remove the chicken from the refrigerator and let it come to room temperature.

3. Place the chicken in a baking dish. Season the tomatoes with salt and pepper and place them in the baking dish. Cover the dish with aluminum foil, place it in the oven, and roast for 25 minutes. Remove the foil and continue roasting until the chicken is cooked through, about 25 minutes. Remove from the oven and let the chicken rest for 10 minutes before serving.

Lemon & Garlic Shrimp

INGREDIENTS

2 TABLESPOONS OLIVE OIL

1 LB. SHRIMP, PEELED
AND DEVEINED

8 GARLIC CLOVES, MINCED

½ TEASPOON LEMON-PEPPER
SEASONING

1½ TABLESPOONS FRESH
LEMON JUICE

1 TABLESPOON FINELY CHOPPED
FRESH PARSLEY, FOR GARNISH

1 RED CHILI PEPPER, STEMMED,
SEEDS AND RIBS REMOVED, AND
SLICED THIN, FOR GARNISH

DIRECTIONS

1. Place the olive oil in a large skillet and warm it over
    medium heat. When the oil starts to shimmer, add the
    shrimp and cook, without stirring, for 3 minutes. Remove
    the shrimp from the pan with a slotted spoon and set
    them aside.

2. Reduce the heat to medium-low and add the garlic
    and lemon-pepper seasoning. Cook until the garlic has
    browned, about 2 minutes. Return the shrimp to the
    pan and cooked until warmed through, about 1 minute.
    To serve, sprinkle the lemon juice over the shrimp and
    garnish with the parsley and chili pepper.

Sautéed Radicchio with Beans, Parmesan & Balsamic

YIELD: **4 SERVINGS**

ACTIVE TIME: **1 HOUR**

TOTAL TIME: **24 HOURS**

INGREDIENTS

⅔ CUP DRIED CHICKPEAS, SOAKED OVERNIGHT

1 TABLESPOON OLIVE OIL

1 SMALL HEAD OF RADICCHIO, CORED AND SLICED THIN

1 SHALLOT, MINCED

1 GARLIC CLOVE, MINCED

¼ CUP WHITE WINE

¼ CUP VEGETABLE STOCK (SEE PAGE 125)

½ TEASPOON FINELY CHOPPED FRESH THYME

SALT AND PEPPER, TO TASTE

PARMESAN CHEESE, GRATED, FOR GARNISH

BALSAMIC VINEGAR, TO TASTE

DIRECTIONS

1. Drain the chickpeas. Place them in a large saucepan, cover them with water, and bring to a boil. Reduce the heat so that the beans simmer and cook until tender, about 45 minutes. Drain and let the chickpeas cool.

2. Place the oil in a skillet and warm over medium heat. When the oil starts to shimmer, add the radicchio and sauté until it starts to wilt and brown, about 5 minutes. Stir in the shallot and garlic and sauté until the garlic starts to brown, about 1 minute. Deglaze the pan with the wine and stock.

3. Add the chickpeas to the radicchio mixture along with the thyme. Season the mixture with salt and pepper, cook until almost all of the liquid has evaporated, and then remove the pan from heat. Top with Parmesan and balsamic vinegar and serve.

NOTE: If you have an infused balsamic vinegar, this dish is a perfect opportunity to break it out.

Bamies

INGREDIENTS

OLIVE OIL, AS NEEDED

1 ONION, CHOPPED

1 LB. OKRA, RINSED WELL
AND CHOPPED

1 POTATO, PEELED AND MINCED

1 GARLIC CLOVE, MINCED

2 TOMATOES, CHOPPED

3 TABLESPOONS WHITE WINE

½ CUP VEGETABLE STOCK (SEE
PAGE 125)

2 TABLESPOONS FINELY CHOPPED
FRESH PARSLEY

2 TEASPOONS SUGAR

SALT, TO TASTE

FETA CHEESE, CRUMBLED,
FOR GARNISH

DIRECTIONS

1. Place the olive oil in a large skillet and warm it over
    medium heat. When the oil starts to shimmer, add the
    onion and sauté until it starts to brown, about 8 minutes.
    Add the okra and potato and cook, stirring continuously,
    until they start to soften, about 5 minutes.

2. Add the garlic and cook for 1 minute. Stir in the tomatoes,
    wine, stock, parsley, and sugar and cook until the
    tomatoes have completely collapsed and the okra and
    potato are tender, about 8 minutes. Season with salt,
    garnish with feta, and serve.

Veal Scallopini

INGREDIENTS

½ CUP ALL-PURPOSE FLOUR

½ TEASPOON FRESHLY GRATED NUTMEG

SALT AND PEPPER, TO TASTE

2 TABLESPOONS UNSALTED BUTTER

1 LB. VEAL CUTLETS, POUNDED THIN

½ CUP CHICKEN STOCK (SEE PAGE 109)

¼ CUP PITTED AND SLICED GREEN OLIVES

ZEST AND JUICE OF 1 LEMON

DIRECTIONS

1. Warm a large cast-iron skillet over medium heat for 5 minutes.

2. Place the flour, nutmeg, salt, and pepper on a large plate and stir to combine.

3. Place the butter in the pan. When it starts to sizzle, dredge the veal in the seasoned flour until it is coated lightly on both sides. Working in batches, place the veal in the skillet and cook for about 1 minute on each side, until browned and the juices run clear. Set the cooked veal aside.

4. Deglaze the pan with the stock. Add the olives, lemon zest, and lemon juice, stir to combine, and cook until heated through. To serve, plate the veal and pour the pan sauce over each cutlet.

NOTE: If you are not a fan of veal, or are simply looking to switch things up, this same preparation will work just as well with chicken cutlets, albeit with a slightly longer cooking time for the meat.

YIELD: **4 SERVINGS**

ACTIVE TIME: **20 MINUTES**

TOTAL TIME: **1 HOUR**

Eggplant Parmesan

INGREDIENTS

1 LARGE EGGPLANT

SALT, TO TASTE

2 TABLESPOONS OLIVE OIL

1 CUP ITALIAN BREAD CRUMBS

½ CUP GRATED PARMESAN CHEESE

1 EGG, BEATEN

MARINARA SAUCE (SEE PAGE 67), AS NEEDED

2 GARLIC CLOVES, MINCED

½ LB. SHREDDED MOZZARELLA CHEESE

FRESH BASIL, FINELY CHOPPED, FOR GARNISH

DIRECTIONS

1. Preheat the oven to 350°F. Trim the top and bottom off the eggplant and slice it into ¼-inch-thick slices. Put the slices on paper towels in a single layer, sprinkle salt over them, and let them rest for about 15 minutes. Turn the slices over, sprinkle salt over the other sides, and let them rest for another 15 minutes. Rinse the eggplant and pat dry with paper towels.

2. Drizzle the oil over a baking sheet. In a shallow bowl, combine the bread crumbs and Parmesan cheese. Put the beaten egg in another shallow bowl. Dip the slices of eggplant in the egg and then in the bread crumb-and-cheese mixture until both sides are coated. Place the breaded slices on the baking sheet.

3. When all of the eggplant has been breaded, place it in the oven and bake for 10 minutes. Remove, turn the slices over, and bake for another 10 minutes. Remove the eggplant from the oven and let it cool slightly.

4. Place a layer of sauce in a square 8-inch baking dish or a cast-iron skillet and stir in the garlic. Lay some of the eggplant on top of the sauce, top them with more sauce, and then arrange the remaining eggplant on top. Sprinkle the mozzarella over the eggplant.

5. Place the dish in the oven and bake for about 30 minutes, until the sauce is bubbling and the cheese is golden brown. Remove from the oven and let rest for 10 minutes before serving with additional Marinara Sauce and garnishing with fresh basil.

Goulash

INGREDIENTS

2 TABLESPOONS OLIVE OIL

3 LBS. BEEF CHUCK, TRIMMED

3 YELLOW ONIONS, CHOPPED

2 CARROTS, PEELED AND CHOPPED

2 BELL PEPPERS, STEMMED,
SEEDS AND RIBS REMOVED,
AND CHOPPED

1 TEASPOON CARAWAY SEEDS

¼ CUP ALL-PURPOSE FLOUR

3 TABLESPOONS SWEET
HUNGARIAN PAPRIKA

3 TABLESPOONS TOMATO PASTE

2 GARLIC CLOVES, MINCED

1 TEASPOON SUGAR

SALT AND PEPPER, TO TASTE

3 CUPS VEGETABLE STOCK (SEE
PAGE 125)

1 CUP SOUR CREAM

DIRECTIONS

1. Place the oil in a Dutch oven and warm it over medium heat. When the oil starts to shimmer, add the meat in batches and cook until it is browned all over, making sure not to crowd the pan. Remove the browned beef and set aside.

2. Reduce the heat to medium-low. Let the pot cool for 2 minutes and then add the onions, carrots, and peppers. Stir to coat the vegetables with the pan drippings and sauté the vegetables until they are golden brown, about 10 minutes. Stir in the caraway seeds and cook until they are fragrant, about 1 minute.

3. Stir in the flour, paprika, tomato paste, garlic, sugar, salt, and pepper, add the stock, and use a wooden spoon to scrape up any browned bits from the bottom of the pan.

4. Bring the goulash to a boil, reduce the heat, and let it simmer until it thickens slightly, about 10 minutes. Return the meat to the Dutch oven, cover, and simmer over low heat until the meat is very tender, about 2 hours.

5. To serve, stir the sour cream into the goulash.

YIELD: **4 SERVINGS**

ACTIVE TIME: **30 MINUTES**

TOTAL TIME: **1 HOUR**

Bigos

INGREDIENTS

2 TABLESPOONS OLIVE OIL

½ LB. KIELBASA, DICED

6½ TABLESPOONS UNSALTED BUTTER

2 LARGE ONIONS, DICED

SALT AND PEPPER, TO TASTE

1½ LBS. GREEN CABBAGE, CORED AND DICED

DIRECTIONS

1. Place the olive oil in a large skillet and warm it over medium heat. When the oil starts to shimmer, add the kielbasa and cook, stirring occasionally, until it starts to brown, about 5 minutes. Use a slotted spoon to transfer the kielbasa to a small bowl.

2. Add 3 tablespoons of the butter to the skillet. When it has melted and stopped foaming, add the onions and a couple pinches of salt and sauté until the onion is soft, about 10 minutes. Add another 3 tablespoons of the butter, the cabbage, a few more pinches of salt, and a few pinches of pepper and stir to combine. When the mixture starts sizzling, cover the pan and reduce the heat to medium-low. Cook, stirring occasionally, until the cabbage is tender and brown, 25 to 30 minutes.

3. Stir in the remaining butter and the kielbasa. Cook until warmed through, season to taste, and serve.

Chili con Carne

INGREDIENTS

1½ LBS. GROUND BEEF

1 (28 OZ.) CAN OF CRUSHED SAN MARZANO TOMATOES, WITH THEIR LIQUID

1 RED BELL PEPPER, STEMMED, SEEDS AND RIBS REMOVED, AND CHOPPED

2 SMALL YELLOW ONIONS, CHOPPED, PLUS MORE FOR GARNISH

4 GARLIC CLOVES, MINCED

1 JALAPEÑO PEPPER, STEMMED, SEEDS AND RIBS REMOVED, AND MINCED

1 LB. PINTO BEANS, SOAKED OVERNIGHT AND DRAINED

¼ CUP FINELY CHOPPED FRESH CILANTRO, PLUS MORE FOR GARNISH

¼ CUP HOT SAUCE

2 TABLESPOONS CHILI POWDER

1 TABLESPOON BLACK PEPPER

1 TABLESPOON KOSHER SALT

2 TABLESPOONS GARLIC POWDER

⅓ CUP CUMIN

1 TABLESPOON MADRAS CURRY POWDER

1 TABLESPOON DRIED OREGANO

CHEDDAR CHEESE, GRATED, FOR GARNISH

DIRECTIONS

1. Place the ground beef in a Dutch oven and cook over medium heat, breaking it up with a fork as it cooks, until it is browned, about 8 minutes.

2. Drain the fat from the beef, add all of the remaining ingredients, except for the garnishes, and stir to combine. Bring to a boil, reduce heat so that the chili gently simmers, and cook until the beans are fork-tender and the flavor is to your liking, 3 to 4 hours.

3. Ladle into warmed bowls and garnish with the cheddar cheese and the additional onion and cilantro.

Chicken with 40 Cloves

INGREDIENTS

8 BONELESS, SKINLESS
CHICKEN THIGHS

SALT AND PEPPER, TO TASTE

OLIVE OIL, AS NEEDED

8 WHITE OR BABY BELLA
MUSHROOMS, QUARTERED

40 GARLIC CLOVES

⅓ CUP DRY VERMOUTH

¾ CUP CHICKEN STOCK (SEE
PAGE 109)

1 TABLESPOON UNSALTED BUTTER

1 TABLESPOON FINELY CHOPPED
FRESH TARRAGON

DIRECTIONS

1. Preheat the oven to 350°F. Generously season the chicken with salt and pepper and place a Dutch oven over high heat. Add the chicken in one layer, cooking in batches if necessary. Although oil is not necessary when cooking chicken thighs, if the pan looks too dry for your liking add a drizzle of olive oil. When brown on one side, flip to the other side and repeat. Transfer to a plate when fully browned but before they are cooked through.

2. Put the mushrooms in the pot and sauté over medium heat, stirring occasionally, until they are browned all over, about 10 minutes. Add the garlic and sauté for 1 minute.

3. Stir in the vermouth and stock, scrape the browned bits from the bottom of the pot, and then return the chicken to the Dutch oven.

4. Cover the Dutch oven with a lid, place the pot in the oven, and let the chicken braise until the chicken thighs are tender and cooked through, about 25 minutes.

5. Remove from the oven and transfer the chicken and mushrooms to a separate plate. With a fork or large spoon, mash about half of the garlic cloves and stir to incorporate them into the pan sauce. If the sauce is still thin, place the pot over medium-high heat and cook until it has reduced. Return the chicken and mushrooms to the pot, reduce the heat, and cook until warmed through.

6. Stir in the butter and tarragon, season to taste, and serve.

YIELD: **4 SERVINGS**

ACTIVE TIME: **40 MINUTES**

TOTAL TIME: **2 HOURS**

Ratatouille

INGREDIENTS

⅓ CUP OLIVE OIL

6 GARLIC CLOVES, MINCED

1 EGGPLANT, SLICED

2 ZUCCHINI, SLICED INTO
HALF-MOONS

2 BELL PEPPERS, STEMMED,
SEEDS AND RIBS REMOVED,
AND CHOPPED

4 TOMATOES, SEEDED
AND SLICED

SALT AND PEPPER, TO TASTE

DIRECTIONS

1. Place a large cast-iron skillet over medium-high heat and add half of the olive oil. When the oil starts to shimmer, add the garlic and eggplant and sauté until pieces start to sizzle, about 2 minutes.

2. Reduce the heat to medium and stir in the zucchini, peppers, and remaining oil. Cover the skillet and cook, stirring occasionally, until the eggplant, zucchini, and peppers are almost tender, about 15 minutes.

3. Add the tomatoes, stir to combine, and cook until the eggplant, zucchini, and peppers are tender and the tomatoes have collapsed, about 25 minutes. Remove the skillet from heat, season with salt and pepper, and allow to sit for at least 1 hour. Reheat before serving.

NOTE: Grilled sausage is a wonderful addition if you're looking to add a little protein to this dish.

YIELD: **6 SERVINGS**

ACTIVE TIME: **15 MINUTES**

TOTAL TIME: **45 MINUTES**

Caprese Chicken

INGREDIENTS

1 GARLIC CLOVE, MINCED

1 TEASPOON DRIED OREGANO

1 TEASPOON GARLIC POWDER

SALT AND PEPPER, TO TASTE

2 TABLESPOONS OLIVE OIL

2 LBS. BONELESS, SKINLESS
CHICKEN BREASTS, HALVED
ALONG THEIR EQUATORS

1 LB. TOMATOES, SLICED

1 LB. FRESH MOZZARELLA CHEESE,
DRAINED AND SLICED

LEAVES FROM 1 BUNCH OF
FRESH BASIL

BALSAMIC GLAZE, FOR GARNISH

DIRECTIONS

1. Preheat the oven to 375°F. Place the minced garlic, oregano, garlic powder, salt, and pepper in a bowl and stir to combine. Place 1 tablespoon of the olive oil and the chicken breasts in a bowl and toss to coat. Dredge the chicken breasts in the garlic-and-spice mixture and set them aside.

2. Coat the bottom of a large cast-iron skillet with the remaining oil and warm it over medium-high heat. When the oil starts to shimmer, add the chicken in batches and sear for 1 minute on each side.

3. When all of the chicken has been seared, place half of the breasts in an even layer on the bottom of the skillet. Top with two-thirds of the tomatoes and mozzarella and half of the basil leaves. Place the remaining chicken breasts on top in an even layer and cover it with the remaining tomatoes, mozzarella, and basil.

4. Place the skillet in the oven and cook until the interior temperature of the chicken breasts is 165°F, about 15 minutes. Remove the skillet from the oven and let rest for 10 minutes. Drizzle the balsamic glaze over the top and serve.

Swedish Meatballs

INGREDIENTS

4 TABLESPOONS UNSALTED BUTTER

1 SMALL ONION, CHOPPED

¼ CUP MILK

1 LARGE EGG

1 LARGE EGG YOLK

3 SLICES OF WHITE BREAD

¼ TEASPOON ALLSPICE

¼ TEASPOON FRESHLY GRATED NUTMEG

PINCH OF GROUND GINGER

¾ LB. GROUND PORK

½ LB. GROUND BEEF

SALT AND PEPPER, TO TASTE

¼ CUP ALL-PURPOSE FLOUR

2½ CUPS CHICKEN STOCK (SEE PAGE 109)

½ CUP HEAVY CREAM

DIRECTIONS

1. Preheat the broiler to high, position a rack so that the tops of the meatballs will be approximately 6 inches below the broiler, and line a rimmed baking sheet with aluminum foil.

2. Place 2 tablespoons of the butter in a large skillet and melt it over medium-high heat. Add the onion and sauté until it is translucent, about 3 minutes. Remove the pan from heat and set it aside.

3. Place the milk, egg, and egg yolk in a mixing bowl and stir to combine. Tear the bread into small pieces and add them to mixing bowl along with the allspice, nutmeg, and ginger. Stir in the pork, beef, and the onion, season the mixture with salt and pepper, and stir until thoroughly combined. Working with wet hands, form the mixture into 1½-inch meatballs, arrange them on the baking sheet, and spray the tops with cooking spray.

4. Place the meatballs in the oven and broil until browned all over, turning them as they cook. Remove the meatballs from the oven and set them aside.

5. Place the remaining butter in the skillet and melt it over low heat. Stir in the flour, cook for 2 minutes while stirring constantly, and then raise the heat to medium-high. Stir in the stock and cream and bring to a boil.

6. Add the meatballs to the sauce, reduce the heat to low, cover the pan, and simmer, turning the meatballs occasionally, until they are cooked through, about 15 minutes. Season with salt and pepper and serve.

METRIC CONVERSIONS

U.S. Measurement	Approximate Metric Liquid Measurement	Approximate Metric Dry Measurement
1 teaspoon	5 ml	5 g
1 tablespoon or ½ ounce	15 ml	14 g
1 ounce or ⅛ cup	30 ml	29 g
¼ cup or 2 ounces	60 ml	57 g
⅓ cup	80 ml	76 g
½ cup or 4 ounces	120 ml	113 g
⅔ cup	160 ml	151 g
¾ cup or 6 ounces	180 ml	170 g
1 cup or 8 ounces or ½ pint	240 ml	227 g
1½ cups or 12 ounces	350 ml	340 g
2 cups or 1 pint or 16 ounces	475 ml	454 g
3 cups or 1½ pints	700 ml	680 g
4 cups or 2 pints or 1 quart	950 ml	908 g

INDEX

ABOUT CIDER MILL PRESS
BOOK PUBLISHERS

Good ideas ripen with time. From seed to harvest, Cider Mill Press brings fine reading, information, and entertainment together between the covers of its creatively crafted books. Our Cider Mill bears fruit twice a year, publishing a new crop of titles each spring and fall.

"Where Good Books Are Ready for Press"

Visit us online at
cidermillpress.com
or write to us at
PO Box 454
12 Spring St.
Kennebunkport, Maine 04046

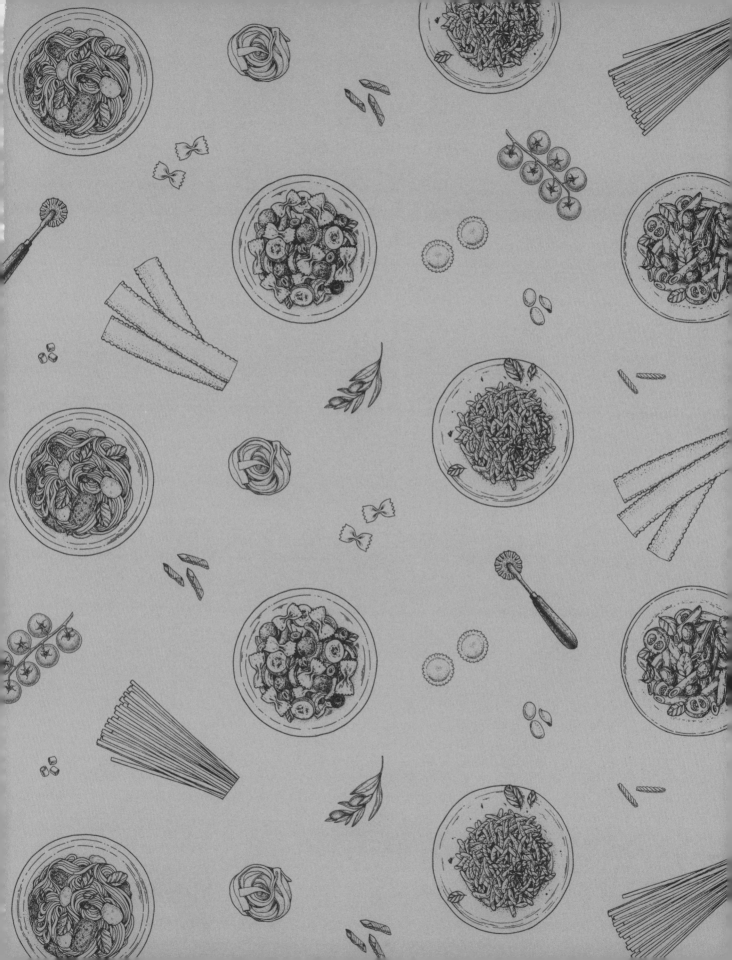